Philip William Stanhope

Official Papers, Letters and Notes

relating to the war record of P.W. Stanhope, major and brevet

lieutenant-colonel, U.S. army

Philip William Stanhope

Official Papers, Letters and Notes
relating to the war record of P.W. Stanhope, major and brevet lieutenant-colonel, U.S. army

ISBN/EAN: 9783337091934

Printed in Europe, USA, Canada, Australia, Japan

Cover: Foto ©ninafisch / pixelio.de

More available books at **www.hansebooks.com**

OFFICIAL PAPERS

LETTERS AND NOTES

RELATING TO THE WAR RECORD OF

P. W. STANHOPE,

MAJOR AND BREVET LIEUTENANT-COLONEL,

U. S. ARMY.

Recognizing the uncertainty of life, and desiring to leave a record of so much of my military career as is possible for me to prepare at this time, I have gathered into book form such of my official, and other papers, as were not lost in the fire that destroyed most of my papers and all of my personal property.

I do this in the hope that, at some distant time, when I shall be dead, my family may read this book with that interest a long interval of years gives to the personal history of a parent who gave a large portion of his life to the service of his Country, and bore a good share of the perils and sufferings incident to war.

With this object in view this book is affectionately dedicated.

PHILIP W. STANHOPE,

MAJOR AND BREVET LIEUTENANT-COLONEL, U. S. ARMY.

Kenton County, Kentucky.

TO
MY CHILDREN.

OFFICIAL PAPERS, LETTERS AND NOTES.

OFFICIAL PAPERS.

WAR DEPARTMENT,
WASHINGTON, JUNE 18, 1861.

SIR:—You are hereby informed that the President of the United States has appointed you Captain in the Twelfth Regiment of Infantry, in the service of the United States, to rank as such from the fourteenth day of May, one thousand eight hundred and sixty one. Should the Senate, at their next session, advise and consent thereto, you will be commissioned accordingly.

Immediately on receipt hereof, please to communicate to this Department, through the Adjutant General's Office, your acceptance or non-acceptance of said appointment; and, with your letter of acceptance, return to the Adjutant General of the Army the Oath herewith enclosed, properly filled up, Subscribed and Attested, reporting at the same time your Age, Residence when appointed, and the State in which you were born.

Should you accept, you will at once report, in person, for orders, to your Colonel, (Colonel W. B. Franklin) at Fort Hamilton, New York Harbor, N. Y.

CAPTAIN P. W. STANHOPE,   SIMON CAMERON,
  12th Regiment Infantry.   Secretary of War.

Extract from Major H. B. Glitz' report of the Battle of Gaines' Mill, fought on the 27th day of June, 1862.

*   *   *   *   *

I cannot speak in too high terms of the steadiness, cool courage and gallant conduct of both my officers and men. Although their first battle, they behaved like tried Soldiers and I feel it an honor to have been their commander on so well a contested field of battle.

I can hardly express my admiration of the gallant bearing of Captains Blunt, Wister and Sergeant, Lieutenants Carter, Stacey, Franklin, H. E. Smith, Parker, Burnett, Hecksher and Tracey, Sergeants Evans, Eggemeyer, Lamoinne, Keller, Ochiltree, Urmston, Meeker, Wagner and Thierman.

Conspicuous even among these brave officers I must not fail to mention Captains READ, WINTHROP and STANHOPE and Lieutenant VAN RENSSELLIER.

I received, throughout the day, the most valuable assistance from my Quarter-Master, Lieutenant Franklin, and my Acting Adjutant, Lieutenant Stacey.

Very respectfully your obedient servant,   H. B. CLITZ,
                                              Major 12th Infantry, Commanding.
LIEUTENANT S. VAN RENSSELLIER,
  Acting Assistant Adjutant General, 1st Brigade, Sykes' Division.

ASHTABULA, AUGUST 9, 1862.

CAPTAIN P. W. STANHOPE:

Dear Sir:—Your plan is a very excellent one. The regiments ought to be placed under the charge of those, and those only, who have had experience and have been under fire. I have no doubt that Governor Tod will be strongly of this opinion and, as he has the entire control of the volunteers of the State, he must be apprised of all the opportunities for detailing experienced officers to the regiments. I think you had better write to him on the subject.

I was exceedingly gratified to hear of your good conduct on the field, as well as your final escape without more serious injuries. Accept the kind regards of Mrs. Wade and myself.
Yours Truly,
B. F. WADE.

CINCINNATI, AUGUST 26, 1862.

EX-GOVERNOR DENNISON,
Columbus, Ohio:

Dear Sir:—I beg to introduce to you Captain P. W. Stanhope, of the 12th Regiment, Regular Army. I have known him for several years as a gentleman of first-rate character and intelligence. He is well and favorably known in this city.

He passed through the recent seven-days battles before Richmond with distinction and bears the marks of them.

Should he succeed in the object for which he visits Columbus, he will doubtless do credit to the State. With high respect, Yours.
JOHN W ELLIS.

CINCINNATI, AUGUST 28, 1862

To HIS EXCELLENCY, DAVID TOD,
Governor of Ohio:

Dear Sir:—I take pleasure in recommending Captain P. W. Stanhope, of the Regular Army, for the position of Colonel of one of the new regiments, should there be any vacancy. He was wounded in one of the recent battles before Richmond, but has now sufficiently recovered to take a command, and is in every way worthy and competent.
Yours truly,
W. H. CLEMENT.

CINCINNATI, AUGUST 29, 1862.

GOVERNOR TOD,

My Dear Sir:—Permit me to introduce to your special notice Captain P. W. Stanhope, of the 12th United States Infantry. Captain Stanhope fought in the batties before Richmond most gallantly, and was grievously wounded on the field. If you can avail yourself of his services to command one of the new regiments, you would confer an appointment upon a well-spirited soldier of most competent military skill and experience, besides rewarding an Ohio man true to his country.

Very Truly,
B. STORER.

HEAD-QUARTERS UNITED STATES FORCES,
CINCINNATI, SEPTEMBER 5, 1862.

CIRCULAR.

Captain P. W. Stanhope, 12th United States Infantry, is hereby assigned to the command of the Volunteer forces collected for the defense of the cities of Cincinnati, Covington and Newport, to rank as Brigadier General. By order of

L. WALLACE,
Major General.

JAMES F. TROTH,
Captain and A. D. C.

HEAD-QUARTERS UNITED STATES FORCES,
SEPTEMBER 9, 1862.

GENERAL:

I have the honor to report that I shall go over to Cincinnati to report to General Wright. If you desire my services to-day, please send word to the Burnet House. If General Wright orders me back to my post, a telegram sent to Lafayette, Indiana, will command my presence. I shall be happy to serve you in any position you may choose to assign me, if leave can be obtained from the War Department.

I am, General, very respectfully, your most obedient servant,

H. KENASTON,
1st Lieut. 11th U. S. Inf.

To Brigadier General STANHOPE,
Com'g U. S. Forces for defense of Covington.

HEAD-QUARTERS FIRST DIVISION U. S. FORCES.
FORT MITCHEL, KY., September 17. 1862.

GENERAL:

It is reported the Rebels are advancing, and their advance guard up to or on this side of Florence; have your command in readiness. Respectfully,

A. J. SMITH,
Brig. Gen'l Com'g.

General P. W. STANHOPE,
Com'g 3d Brigade, 1st Division.

OFFICIAL PAPERS.

HEAD-QUARTERS U. S. FORCES,
Covington, Ky., September 24, 1862.

General:
You will cause to be delivered to Captain W. W. Andrew, 21st Indiana Battery, five twelve-pounder guns and caissons which were under charge of a detachment of the 9th Ohio Battery. By order of

Brig. Gen'l A. J. SMITH,
R. F. Rogers, A. D. C.

To P. W. Stanhope,
Brig. Gen'l Com'g.

Ashtabula, October 13, 1862.
Captain P. W. Stanhope,

Dear Sir:—Immediately on the receipt of your letter I wrote to the President as strong a letter as I was able and enclosed the letter of General Wallace. Your testimonials are all that a man could ask, and are such as you may justly be proud of. I am exceedingly gratified to think that I was instrumental in procuring your first appointment, and hope I may be equally successful in obtaining your promotion.

Our kind regards to you. Yours truly,

B. F. WADE.

HEAD-QUARTERS U. S. FORCES,
Columbus, Ohio, November 19, 1862.
Hon. E. M. Stanton, Secretary of War,

Sir:—I have the honor to recommend Captain P. W. Stanhope, 12th U. S. Infantry, to the President for promotion to the rank of Brigadier General of Volunteers.

Captain Stanhope commanded one of the brigades, under my orders, collected for the defense of Kentucky from General E. Kirby Smith. He was one of the most active, intelligent and reliable brigade commanders within my notice. His untiring exertions and attention were of the utmost value in bringing his command to a state of efficiency far above that of the other brigades present.

Although but just paroled from Libby Prison, and seriously wounded, as soon as exchanged he took the field, and remained actively engaged in the discipline and instruction of his brigade, and construction of lines of defense, until the enemy had left his front, when his wounds breaking out compelled his relief from command.

This young officer is greatly deserving this promotion, and I take pleasure in commending him to the favorable notice of the Honorable Secretary of War.

Very respectfully, your obedient servant,

LEWIS WALLACE, Major General.

OFFICIAL PAPERS.

CINCINNATI, June 16, 1863.

MY DEAR BROTHER:

It affords me pleasure to introduce to you my friend, Captain P. W. Stanhope, 12th Infantry, U. S. A., now mustering and disbursing officer at this point. Since Captain S. was badly wounded at the battle of Gaines' Mills, he has been detached for service in the above department. During the celebrated raid last summer he offered his services, and acted in command of a brigade in so happy a manner as to gain the respect of our citizens and the full confidence of his troops. As a gentleman and officer he is worthy of your high consideration and regard.

Very truly, &c., E. B. DENNISON.

Gov. W. DENNISON,
Columbus, Ohio.

HEAD-QUARTERS, DISTRICT OF OHIO,

CINCINNATI, OHIO, July 12, 1863.

CAPTAIN:

I desire to write your father this morning, but do not know his first name. Will you be so kind as to furnish it to me? Please also designate a time when I can see you. I desire to learn all the particulars of the death of your brother. He was one of the noblest, most gallant fellows I ever knew, and my best friend.

I am, Captain, very respectfully, your obedient servant,

H. L. BURNETT,

Captain P. W. STANHOPE, Major and Acting J. A.
U. S. A. Cincinnati, O.

WAR DEPARTMENT, ADJUTANT GENERAL'S OFFICE,

WASHINGTON, August 20, 1863.

SPECIAL ORDERS, No. 371. (Extract.)

5. Captain Philip W. Stanhope, 12th U. S. Infantry, will proceed without delay to Columbus, Ohio, and relieve Colonel Horace Brooks, 4th U. S. Artillery, in the duties of Superintendent of Volunteer Recruiting Service, and Chief Mustering and Disbursing Officer at that place. On being relieved Colonel Brooks will immediately join the head-quarters of his regiment at Fort Washington, Md.

By order of the Secretary of War,

E. D. TOWNSEND,

CAPT. STANHOPE, Assistant Adjutant General.
Cincinnati, Ohio.

OFFICIAL PAPERS.

HEAD-QUARTERS, PORT ROYAL,
MAY 26, 1864.

SPECIAL ORDERS. No. 15.   (Extract.)

1. Captain Stanhope's detachment of five hundred (500) men will be immediately turned over to their proper commands, after having been relieved by the Veteran Reserve Corps.

Captain Stanhope will not be relieved from the duties of Provost Marshal of the Town proper, but will exercise the functions of that office, giving all necessary instructions to the new guard, and assistance to the U. S. Provost Marshal, Captain Hoysradt. By order of

BRIGADIER GENERAL J. J. ABERCROMBIE,
ROBERT L. ORR, Captain and A. A. A. G.

HEAD-QUARTERS U. S. FORCES,
WHITE HOUSE, VA., June 20, 1864.

GENERAL ORDERS, No 10.

The undersigned hereby relinquishes the command of the troops at this station to Brigadier General George W. Getty.

In doing so he avails himself of this opportunity of expressing his high appreciation of the services of his staff in their respective positions; tendering his sincere thanks to Captain Charles Babcock and the officers of the navy for the very efficient aid and support to the land forces in the persistent attack on the post by the enemy to-day.

J. J. ABERCROMBIE,
Brigadier General.

To Captain P. W. STANHOPE,
Provost Marshal.

ROXBURY, July 18, 1864.

DEAR SIR:

I have the honor to acknowledge the reception of your favor of the 11th inst. Apart from the kind congratulations it contained and the handsome tribute to my husband's success, which were very highly appreciated, it gave me sincere pleasure to hear of your own welfare, as I had never learned anything respecting you since our agreeable residence in Cleveland, except through your kind attention to my son shortly after.

If you should ever visit Boston, you must not forget to come and see us. I feel assured Captain Winslow will be much gratified by your remembrance, and equally pleased with myself to renew your acquaintance. Very truly yours,

CATHARINE A. WINSLOW.

Captain P. W. STANHOPE,
12th U. S. Infantry.

CINCINNATI, September 26, 1864.

GOVERNOR:

My friend, Captain P. W. Stanhope, U. S. A., is, I learn to-day, willing to command one of the new Ohio regiments. I, therefore, without his knowledge, take great pleasure in indorsing him to you as a gentleman and a most competent soldier. In his appointment Ohio will give opportunity to another son to still advance her position in the war to perpetuate the Republic. Cordially and truly,

T. J. GALLAGHER.

His Excellency, Governor BROUGH,
    Columbus, Ohio.

CINCINNATI, September 26, 1864.

GOVERNOR:

I have the pleasure of introducing to your acquaintance and favorable attention Captain P. W. Stanhope, of the 12th U. S. Infantry. I have known Captain Stanhope for some years as a citizen of this place. He went into the service soon after the breaking out of the rebellion, and went through all the battles on the Peninsula in 1862, until he was severely wounded at the battle of Gaines' Mills. As soon as fit for active duty, he again returned to his command, and is now serving under General Grant near Petersburg, where he commands his own and another regiment of regulars (the 14th.) I am informed that he is solicitous of an appointment as colonel of one of our new regiments, for which position, from my personal knowledge of his capacity, I take great pleasure in recommending him. Very truly your obedient servant,

STANLEY MATTHEWS.

His Excellency, JNO. BROUGH, Governor, &c.

HEAD-QUARTERS, NORTHERN DEPARTMENT,
    CINCINNATI, OHIO, October 12, 1864.

Hon. E. M. STANTON, Secretary of War:

I beg leave to recommend Captain P. W. Stanhope, of the 12th Infantry, for promotion to the rank of Brigadier General in the Volunteer service.

In 1861 he was commissioned as a captain in the 12th Infantry, and has borne a conspicuous part in the rebellion, in the armies of the East and the West.

At the battle of Gaines' Mills he was especially prominent, his conduct receiving flattering notice in the official report of his commanding officer.

Three times in the course of his service in the rebellion he has commanded a brigade to the satisfaction of his commanding generals, especially at the late fight of the 5th Corps on the Weldon Railroad.

The limits of a testimonial admit of but a brief reference to the services of this young officer,—they have been long and distinguished. He was wounded and left for dead on the field at Gaines' Mills, but is now sufficiently recovered to enable him to perform the duties of his office.

Captain Stanhope is a brave, intelligent officer, and in private life irreproachable. I take great pleasure in commending him to the favorable consideration of the Honorable Secretary of War.

JOSEPH HOOKER,
Major General Com'g.

HEAD-QUARTERS, FIFTY-FIFTH K'Y VOLS., INFANTRY,
COVINGTON, KY., October 15, 1864.

Captain PHILIP W. STANHOPE, 12th U. S. Infantry,

You are hereby directed to take charge of the camp and rendezvous of the 55th Regiment Kentucky Volunteers, and superintend the recruitment, mustering, and organization of said regiment. By order of

G. CLAY SMITH,
Brigadier General Commanding.

HEAD QUARTERS FIRST DIVISION, MILITARY DISTRICT OF KENTUCKY,
LEXINGTON, KY., November 12, 1864.

Colonel STANHOPE, Commanding 55th Kentucky Infantry:

It is understood, by orders from District Head-quarters, you are assigned to this division, and to report by letter. And, if such is the case, the General directs that you do so at once, giving full particulars in regard to the organization of the regiment. Very respectfully, your obedient servant.

J. S. BUTLER,
Assistant Adjutant General.

[Telegram received by Colonel Stanhope at Covington, Ky., November 18, 1864.]
HEAD-QUARTERS, LEXINGTON, KY.,
NOVEMBER 18, 1864.

To Colonel P. W. STANHOPE, Covington:

Report here to-morrow by rail with all the men of your command you have mustered in and armed ready for service. If possible to have horses and horse equipments for them at Covington, do so and bring them. Answer.

By order of Brevet Major General Burbridge.

J. BATES DICKSON,
Captain and A. A. G.

OFFICIAL PAPERS.

HEAD-QUARTERS FIRST DIVISION, MILITARY DISTRICT OF KENTUCKY,
LEXINGTON, November 23, 1864.

Colonel STANHOPE, 55th Kentucky Volunteers:

You will move your command by rail to Nicholasville immediately. Cars are waiting for you at present. As soon as you arrive at Nicholasville you will move to Crab Orchard, via Camp Nelson. Three companies of the 53d Kentucky have been ordered to report to you. Four companies of the 45th Kentucky will report to you as soon as they arrive at Camp Nelson. The three companies of the 53d Kentucky are on the train at depot. The General wishes you to report here before you go to depot. By command of

BRIGADIER GENERAL McLEAN,
J. S. BUTLER, A. A. G.

HEAD-QUARTERS IN THE FIELD,
BARBOURSVILLE, KY., November 27, 1864.

CIRCULAR.

GENERAL ORDERS, No. 3.

The undersigned hereby assumes command of all the forces now at this point, by order of Major-General Burbridge.

The order of march for to-morrow, November 28, will be as follows:

 45th Ky. Vols.
 13th "   "
 12th "   "

The Senior Commissioned Officer will march at 12 o'clock, to-night, and proceed to the ford, cross and march to Cumberland Gap, reporting to General Burbridge at noon, Monday. No straggling will be allowed. Officers of each Command will be held strictly responsible for the proper execution of this order.

P. W. STANHOPE,
Colonel Com'g.

HEAD-QUARTERS FORCES IN THE FIELD.
CUMBERLAND GAP, November 29, 1864.

COL. P. W. STANHOPE, Com'd'g 55th Ky. Mt'd Inf.

COLONEL:—The General Commanding desires me to say to you that in answer to an inquiry from the Officers of your Regiment, in regard to the date of their muster, that it shall be dated back to the time when they were ordered into the field for active service, in obedience to instructions received from the Secretary of War.

I am, very respectfully, your obedient servant,

CHAS. M. KEYSER,
Capt. and A. A. A. G.

HEAD-QUARTERS FORCES IN FIELD.
CUMBERLAND GAP, KY., November 29, 1864.

Asst. Surgeon, J. H. McMAHON, 54th Ky., will report to Colonel Stanhope, commanding Battalion 53rd and 55th Ky. Regiments, for duty.

J. G. HATCHILL,
Surgeon, U. S. A., Surg'n-in-Chief.

Doctor McMahon came recommended to my Regiment by the best Medical Men in the Army, also, by the Examining Board in Louisville.

H. M. BUCKLEY,
Colonel Comd'g 54th Ky.

WAR DEPARTMENT,
WASHINGTON, December 2, 1864.

SIR:— You are hereby informed that the President of the United States has appointed you, for Gallant Services during the operations on the Weldon Railroad, Va., a Major by Brevet, in the service of the United States, to rank as such from the Eighteenth day of August, one thousand eight hundred and sixty-four. Should the Senate, at their next session, advise and consent thereto, you will be commissioned accordingly.

Immediately on receipt hereof, please communicate to this Department, through the Adjutant General of the Army, your acceptance or non-acceptance; and with your letter of acceptance, return the Oath herewith enclosed, properly filled up. Subscribed and Attested, and report your Age, Birthplace and the State of which you were a permanent resident.

E. M. STANTON,
Secretary of War.

Brevet Major PHILIP W. STANHOPE, U. S. Army.
Through Commanding General, Army Potomac.

HEAD-QUARTERS MILITARY DISTRICT OF KENTUCKY,
LEXINGTON, KY., December 16, 1864.

SPECIAL ORDERS, NO. 92.

4. Colonel P. W. Stanhope is assigned to the command of the Camp of Rendezvous, at Covington, Ky., established by Special Orders, No. 26, Par. 5, of date October 5, 1864, from these Head-Quarters, vice G. Clay Smith, relieved.

By Command of Brevet Major-General S. G. Burbridge.

Captain P. W. STANHOPE,   J. BATES DICKSON,
55th Ky., Covington, Ky.   Captain and A. A. G.

HEAD-QUARTERS MILITARY DISTRICT OF KENTUCKY.

LEXINGTON, KY., January 5, 1865.

Colonel P. W. STANHOPE, 55th Ky. Volunteers,

COLONEL:—The General Commanding directs that you mount your command by impressing horses from disloyal citizens. In pressing horses you will be governed by the following instructions:—

No horses must be pressed from Union men, nor can you purchase from them, and any receipts given to such will be worthless.

In pressing horses employ discreet and careful officers, to whom you will give imperative orders to take none but serviceable horses and mares fit for Cavalry use and only from disloyal citizens, to whom you will give disloyal receipts. Every animal so taken shall be valued by the impressing Officer, and the value stated in the receipt; such valuation not to exceed the price being paid by the Government for horses at the time.

In no case will the only remaining horse of a widow or farmer be taken.

Officers must furnish their own horses; they are not allowed to use Government animals.

You will acknowledge the receipt of these instructions, and see that your Officers rigidly adhere to them.

Very respectfully, your obedient servant,

J. BATES DICKSON,
Captain and A. A. G.

HEAD-QUARTERS DEPOT FOR PRISONERS OF WAR.

ELMIRA, N. Y. May 4, 1865.

SPECIAL ORDER, No. 80.   (Extract.)

1. Lieutenant James R. Reid, 10th U. S. Infantry, having been relieved from duty at this Depot by S. O., No. 182, War Dept. A. G. O., dated April 22, 1865, is hereby relieved from duty as Inspector of Prison Camp and Provisional Brigade.

He will turn over to Captain and Brevet Major P. W. Stanhope, 12th U. S. Infantry, all orders, instructions and official papers in his possession, pertaining to his office as Inspector.

2. Captain and Brevet Major P. W. Stanhope, 12th U. S. Infantry, is hereby appointed Inspector of Prison Camp and Provisional Brigade at this Depot, and will be respected accordingly.

By order of Col. B. F. Tracy.

R. J. McKEE,
Lieut. and A. A. A. G.

Captain P. W. STANHOPE,
   12th U. S. Inf., Bvt. Maj. U. S. A.
   Through C. O., Provisional Brigade.

OFFICIAL PAPERS.

HEAD-QUARTERS DEPOT PRISONERS OF WAR,
ELMIRA, N. Y., May 16, 1865.

GENERAL ORDERS, NO. 4.

The troops at this Post will assemble on the parade ground, near Camp Chemung, Wednesday, May 17, 1865, at $3\frac{1}{2}$ o'clock, P. M., for inspection and review.

Commanding Officers will report, with their Commands, to Brevet Major P. W. Stanhope, U. S. A., Acting Asst. Inspector General, for position in line.

By order of Colonel B. F. Tracy.

Major P. W. STANHOPE, U. S. A.,   R. J. McKEE,
A. A. Inspector General.   Lieutenant and A. A. A. G.

HEAD-QUARTERS 1st BATT., 12th U. S. INFANTRY,
ELMIRA, N. Y., July 24, 1865.

BATTALION ORDER, NO. 39.

1. In obedience to Special Order, No. 377, Hd. Qrs. Army A. G. O., Washington, D. C., July 17, 1865, Ext. 2, this Battalion will proceed to Fort Hamilton, New York Harbor, on the afternoon of July 25, 1865. By arrangement with the Acting Asst. Provost Marshal General of this District, the detachment 12th U. S. Infantry, composed of Companies C E F and H, doing duty at Syracuse, N. Y., under command of Captain D. D. Van Valzah, will rejoin the Battalion Head-Quarters, at Binghamton, N. Y., from whence the Battalion will proceed to Jersey City, where water transportation will be provided to Fort Hamilton, New York Harbor.

2. Captain P. W. Stanhope, 12th U. S. Infantry, Brevet Major, U. S. A., being the Senior Officer of the 1st Battalion, 12th U. S. Infantry, present, who marched with it originally from Fort Hamilton, New York Harbor, in 1861, the present Commanding Officer waives rank in his favor, and, accordingly, Brevet Major Stanhope, U. S. A., will assume command of the 1st Battalion, and report with it to the Regimental Commander, at Fort Hamilton, New York Harbor.

3. On the arrival of the Battalion at Fort Hamilton, and after it shall have been marched to its quarters, the undersigned will resume command, unless permanently relieved by competent authority.

A. J. DALLAS,
Capt. 2nd Batt., 12th U. S. Inf., Comd'g 1st Batt.

HEAD-QUARTERS DEPARTMENT VA.,
RICHMOND, September 20, 1865.

DEAR MAJOR:—Please inform me whether Col. Anderson, Lieut. Lamonion and Lieut. Alston, of your Regiment, have yet left here for Fort Hamilton, and if so, on what days they left, respectively.   Truly yours,   ALF. H. TERRY,
Brev. Maj. STANHOPE, U. S. A., Comd'g 12th Inf.   M. G. V.

EXECUTIVE MANSION,
RICHMOND, March 6, 1866.

Major STANHOPE, Commanding at Williamsburg, Va.

Major:—You are aware of the disorganized condition of the Asylum at your place. I learn that the present occupant, or Superintendent, refuses to give possession to the new Board. I considered this subject maturely, and was satisfied of the necessity of a change. May I ask you to remove any difficulties in the way of the new Board, and suppress any violence that may be offered to the exercise of authority by them. I am, &c.,
F. H. PIERPONT,
Governor Va.

WILLIAMSBURG, March 7, 1866.

DEAR MAJOR:—There is no rule equal to Military rule when well administered. Excuse me for saying that "Special Order, No. 42" is a most excellent one in all respects. I informed the "Grammar boys" of it to-day. One of them seemed to think it an infringement of his rights as an American citizen. I commended his spirit, and advised him to proceed, forthwith, to your Head-Quarters, there

"To beard the lion in his den,
The Douglass in his hall."

On reflection, he concluded that "discretion was the better part of valor," and that it would be safer to await for the developments. As a matter of justice to these chaps though, I will say, I never saw but one play marbles on Sunday, and him I have been threatening for six weeks. I had the honor to receive yesterday your message concerning my health, which is better, and I would express my thanks.

With my respects to the gentlemen at your Head-Quarters, I remain,
With much respect, yours sincerely,
BENJ. S. EWELL,
Major P. W. STANHOPE.   Prest. William and Mary College.

STATE OF NEW YORK,
BUREAU OF MILITARY RECORD,
ALBANY, March 30, 1866.

MAJOR:—His Excellency, Governor Fenton, has placed in this Bureau the Guidon of the 56th Regiment, N. Y. Vols., forwarded with your favor, of the 25th inst., and he directs me to acknowledge the same, and to thank you for the attention.
I have the honor to be your obt. servant,

Major P. W. STANHOPE,   L. L. DOTY,
Commanding Post, Norfolk, Va.   Chief of Bureau.

HEAD-QUARTERS DEPARTMENT OF VIRGINIA,
RICHMOND, VA., April 18, 1866.

Brevet Major P. W. STANHOPE, U. S. A.,
Commanding Post, Norfolk, Va.

MAJOR:—I have the honor to acknowledge receipt of your communication, of the 16th inst., reporting concerning the riot at Norfolk, Va., on the occasion of the Negro celebration.

The Commanding General approves the course pursued by you, and the steps which you have taken to secure peace and quiet in the city.

He directs me to say, that in reference to your future action, no precise instructions can be given at present. Although Martial law still prevails in this Department, you are not held responsible for the behavior of any citizen. The good order of the city is primarily in charge of the Civil authorities and it is not expedient for the Military authorities to interfere, unless the Civil authorities are clearly unable to preserve order. If disturbances occur, or are, in your judgment, likely to occur, threatening violence to the Colored people, you will interfere to protect or suppress them. You will ascertain, if possible, the names of the parties who fired upon you and lodge the proper complaint with the Civil authorities, and if no action is taken by them, refer the names to these Head-Quarters.

I am, Major, very respectfully, your obt. servant,
ED. W. SMITH,
Asst. Adj. General.

NORFOLK, VIRGINIA.
MAYOR'S COURT, April 20, 1866.

DEAR SIR:—I have the honor to acknowledge your communication of this date and I assure you it is the occasion of profound regret that there should have been any necessity for such communication.

As soon as you informed me of the occurrence referred to, "I directed the efforts of my police towards a thorough investigation of the matter," and I assure you I will use all the means under my control to discover the offenders and bring them to the punishment they so richly deserve.

At this present I cannot furnish you with the names of guilty parties. I beg you will communicate the knowledge to which you allude.

I have the honor to assure you of my consideration. Your obt. servant,
THOMAS C. TABB,

To Major STANHOPE. Mayor of Norfolk City.

HEAD-QUARTERS DEPARTMENT OF KENTUCKY,
LEXINGTON, KENTUCKY, March 20, 1865.

Hon. E. M. STANTON, Secretary of War.

SIR:—I take pleasure in calling your attention to the services of Capt. P. W. Stanhope, 12th U. S. Infantry, commanding the 55th Kentucky Volunteers.

He reported for duty in this Department, and took command of the 55th Ky. Vols. early in October 1864, and has been serving under my immediate notice from that date, up to the present time.

I have always found him a very prompt, efficient and valuable officer. Upon being ordered to join me at Cumberland Gap in November, 1864, he was placed in command of all the troops then en-route to report to me, and accomplished this duty with great skill and success under serious difficulties. At the crossing of Clinch river ford, at Thornhill Gap, at Holston river, and at Rodgersville he behaved with marked gallantry and credit, and in his subsequent duties as commander of troops engaged in clearing the State of Kentucky from guerrilla bands he displayed great energy and untiring effort, capturing many and driving others beyond the limits of his command, at a season of the year when it was considered nearly impossible to keep troops actively engaged in the field, owing to deep snows and intense cold.

At the time the train from Cynthiana to Lexington was attacked by guerrillas, he was a passenger and prominent in making the small train guard defend the lives of the passengers, and finally repel the attack and save the train and those passengers who had remained by his direction on the train.

I have that knowledge of Colonel Stanhope as an officer, which warrants me in respectfully asking that his many acts of gallantry and ability as a commander of troops in battle and in the field may be recognized at the War Department by a suitable Brevet, and consider him greatly deserving this reward for his services while under my command.
S. G. BURBRIDGE,
Major Gen. Com.

HEAD-QUARTERS DEPARTMENT RENDEZVOUS,
ELMIRA, N. Y. May 24, 1865.

SPECIAL ORDER, No. 157.   (Extract.)

4. Brevet Major P. W. Stanhope, 12th U. S. Infantry, is hereby relieved from duty, at this Post as A. A. Inspector General, and will report for duty to the commanding officer of his battalion at this Post, to enable him to proceed with his battalion to the Head-quarters of his Regiment.

In relieving Major Stanhope, the Colonel Commanding desires to express his entire satisfaction at the manner in which he has performed his official duties while detached at these Head-quarters. By order of Col. J. R. Lewis.
H. H. MOTT, Capt. and A. A. Genl.

To Brevet Major P. W. STANHOPE, Comd. 12th Inft.

OFFICIAL PAPERS.

I certify that on or about the 23rd of November 1864, I was ordered by Brigadier Genl. N. C. McClean to remain at Camp Nelson, Ky., and assist Col. Stanhope, there left in command of provisional brigade collected at Camp Nelson, Ky., to arm and equip all the forces, and forward them to General Burbridge in East Tennessee.

That by order of Genl. McClean, Col. Stanhope was in command of all the forces collected there for that purpose, that he did arm and equip such as required arms and equipment and did take command of them, and march them to the front; I assisting him as an aid to that effect.

M. T. HALL,
Capt. 26th Ky., A. A. I. G.

TREASURY DEPARTMENT,
June 4, 1866.

SIR:—Messrs. J. S. Loomis, Assistant Special Agent of the Treasury Department, and E. R. Potter and S. H. Brown of R. I., visit Norfolk for the prosecution of inquiries with a view to securing to Government, certain property rightfully belonging to it, said to be secreted in that vicinity.

I will thank you to afford them any aid or facilities that you properly can, which will enable them to carry out the objects of their mission, and especially to furnish any guard that may be necessary to protect any property of the character referred to that may be found. Very respectfully,

H. McCULLOCH,
To Bvt. Maj. P. W. STANHOPE, Comdg. &c., Norfolk, Va.   Secy. of the Treasury.

WASHINGTON, June 16, 1866.

MAJOR:—At request of my friend, Col. J. S. Loomis, U. S. Treasury Agent at Richmond, Va., I have sent you the "Army Register" for 1865. Thinking it might be convenient for reference for your friends in the Naval Service, near your present station, I also send you the "Naval Register" for 1866, and will send you the Army Register for the present year, when I have received same from the Public Printer.

Very respectfully,
RICHARD YATES.

Major P. W. STANHOPE, 12th U. S. Infantry,
Commanding, &c., Norfolk, Va.

HEAD-QUARTERS MILITARY DISTRICT OF FORT MONROE,
FORT MONROE, VA., August 16, 1866.

DEAR COLONEL:—Your letters are at hand. I heartily appreciate your congratulations, and would be pleased to be associated with you in future, if possible.

When in Washington I learned that the appointments for field officers of colored Infantry had been decided upon, but that the others are still under consideration, and my advice would be for you to file your application at once. Hoping you will meet with success, I remain, Truly your friend,

NELSON A. MILES,
Major General.

Col. P. W. STANHOPE,
Com'dg Post of Norfolk, Va.

ELMIRA, N. Y., October 9, 1866.

DEAR COLONEL:—I have to acknowledge the receipt, by the hand of Captain Earle, of a cane, which shall be kept in my family, I assure you, as the gift of a brave officer, and as having historic associations. It will afford me pleasure to have it properly mounted, and I beg you to send me an appropriate inscription indicating the vessels of whose timbers it was manufactured.

We were in hopes, all of us, to have taken you by the hand before now, this summer; shall we not have that pleasure during the present delightful "Indian summer?" Yours respectfully,

H. M. PARTRIDGE.

To Col. P. W. STANHOPE, U. S. A.

WAR DEPARTMENT, ADJUTANT GENERAL'S OFFICE,
WASHINGTON, December 1, 1866.

SIR:—I have the honor to inclose to you, herewith, your Commission of Brevet Lieutenant Colonel, the receipt of which please acknowledge.

I am, Sir, very respectfully, your obedient servant,

J. C. KELTON,
Assistant Adjutant General.

Brev't Lieut. Colonel P. W. STANHOPE, U. S. A.

HEAD-QUARTERS DEPARTMENT OF WASHINGTON,
WASHINGTON, D. C., January 8, 1867.

SPECIAL ORDERS, NO. 6. (Extract.)

3. In accordance with instructions from the War Department, A. G. O., dated Washington, January 5, 1867, a "Board of Officers" to consist of

Brevet Major General H. E. Maynadier—Major, 12th U. S. Infantry;
Brevet Lieutenant Colonel P. W. Stanhope—Captain, 12th U. S. Infantry; and
1st Lieutenant Edward Hunter, 12th U. S. Infantry, will convene at 10 o'clock,

A. M., Monday, the 14th of January, at Garrison Head-Quarters in this City, to examine and report upon the qualifications for appointment as 2nd Lieutenant in the U. S. Army of Private John R. Sullivan Company "H," 4th U. S. Artillery. The examination will be of a practical nature, and will be conducted so as to exhibit, as well the character of the soldier, his general intelligence, and his fitness for the position and duties of a Commissioned Officer, as his proficiency in the tactics, in administration, and with regard to other necessary points on military knowledge. His military record will be fully considered, and he will present himself to the Board with Surgeon's Certificate setting forth his physical qualification.

By Command of Brevet Major General Ed. R. S. Canby.

J. H. TAYLOR,
Assistant Adjutant General.

Bvt. Lieut. Col. P. W. STANHOPE, Captain, 12th U. S. Infantry,
Through Head-Quarters, Garrison of Washington.

No. 7. BOWLING GREEN, N. Y., May 21, 1867.

Brevet Lieutenant Colonel P. W. STANHOPE,

COLONEL:—Will you do me the favor to state what your recollection is of the attack and defense of the Post at the White House during my command there.

Please state what available force I had, and the estimated strength of the enemy when the attack commenced and how long it lasted and what measures were adopted for the preservation of General Sheridan's supply-train; whether my Head-Quarters were so located during the attack as to enable me to control the movements of the troops; whether any orders were issued by me at any time which conflicted with the instructions received from time to time from the Commanding General. Perhaps it would be as well to state, what measures you adopted as Provost Marshal, to secure the rebel prisoners turned over to you, and any other remarks which you may deem pertinent to the case.

With much respect, your obedient servant,
J. J. ABERCROMBIE,
Col. and Bvt. Brig. Gen. U. S. A.

WASHINGTON, May 28, 1867.

To THE ADJT. GEN. U. S. ARMY.

GENERAL:—I desire to place upon record an acknowledgement of the services rendered by Capt. P. W. Stanhope, Bvt. Lieut. Col. U. S. A. while serving under my command in the department of the Ohio, in 1862.

When the command of Gen. E. K. Smith advanced into Kentucky and defeated the hastily collected forces under General Nelson at Richmond, there was scarcely an organized command in the State to dispute his march upon Louisville or Cincinnati.

The Western States responded promptly to the call for men, but as these were entirely raw and undisciplined and generally commanded by officers without experience, it became necessary to select competent men, without regard to rank, for temporary command of the brigades into which they were organized. Amongst these officers was Capt. Stanhope, who was placed in command of a brigade and in which he was retained till after the rebel forces withdrew from the front of Cincinnati.

During this time he exhibited great zeal and activity, and did much toward disciplining and giving confidence to the excellent material constituting his brigade.

His services could not be brilliant in this connection, as our forces were held strictly on the defensive, but they were of great value in bringing into shape the raw levies as they arrived, and for such he is deserving the acknowledgement of the Government. I think he is well deserving of a Brevet for his services on that occasion and I shall be glad if it shall be conferred.

I know nothing of his later services, personally, but I understand they were likewise valuable. Very Respectfully, your obedient servant,

H. G. WRIGHT,
Bvt. Major General.

No. 7. BOWLING GREEN, N. Y., May 30, 1867.
To Capt. P. W. STANHOPE, Brvt. Lieut. Col. U. S. A.

MY DEAR COLONEL:—I take great pleasure in stating that you served on my staff during the Campaign on the Peninsula, and rendered me most efficient services while acting as Provost Marshal at Belle-Plain, Port Royal, and the White House, and especially at the latter place where, by your indefatigable exertions in removing General Sheridan's Supply-train across the Pamunkey and beyond the reach of the enemy's guns, you contributed in an eminent degree to its preservation, which of itself, independent of your other duties, should entitle you to great credit.

Yours Truly,

J. J. ABERCROMBIE,
Col. and Bvt. Brig. Gen., U. S. A.

271 VERMONT AVENUE, WASHINGTON, D. C., June 16, 1867.
Bvt. Lieut. Col. P. W. STANHOPE, Capt. 12th Infantry,

Having requested a letter from me, relative to his services whilst under my command, it affords me pleasure to state that I found him on all occasions, intelligent, energetic and efficient in the discharge of his duties.

He behaved with marked gallantry and good conduct at the battle of "Gaines' Mills, on the 27th of June, 1862, and was severely wounded, and taken prisoner, which was the last occasion when he served under my observation.

ROBERT BUCHANAN,
Bvt. Major General, U. S. A.

OFFICIAL PAPERS.

SAINT PAUL, MINN. August 19, 1867.
To Lieut. Col. P. W. STANHOPE, Capt. 12th U. S. Inft.

COLONEL:—Your letter of June 7th has claimed my attention for some weeks, but I have just found time to answer it; duties permitting of no delay having absorbed my time entirely.

I hardly know how to write a letter to do justice to the gallant and dangerous service performed by the line officers like yourself. The limits of a letter will not permit a recapitulation of them all, and a partial one might be unfair by attaching undue importance to those named or convey an impression that they were all.

I hope I may however yet live to put on record what I know of the deeds of the "Regulars," and your own brave conduct on the Weldon R. R. as well as elsewhere will not be left out when that is done. You may rely upon my intention to do it.

Truly Yours,   G. K. WARREN.

DISTRIBUTION OF TROOPS SERVING IN DEPT. OF WASHINGTON.

SEPTEMBER 1, 1867.

Brevet Major General W. H. EMORY, Colonel 5th U. S. Cavalry, Commanding;
HEAD-QUARTERS, WASHINGTON, D. C.

STAFF OFFICERS:

Bvt. Brig. Gen. JOSEPH ROBERTS, Lieut. Col. 4th U. S. Artillery, A. A. A G., A. A. I. G., Commissary of Musters and Discharge Officer.

Bvt. Brig. Gen. J. M. McFERRAN, Deputy Quartermaster General U. S. Army, Chief Quartermaster.

Bvt. Col. GEORGE BELL, Commissary of Subsistence, U. S. A. Chief Commissary.

Bvt. Col. L. A. EDWARDS, Surgeon U. S. Army, Medical Director.

	STATIONS.	COMMANDING OFFICER.	TROOPS.
GARRISON OF WASHINGTON, Lt. Col. G. W. WALLACE, Comdg.	Sedgwick Barracks.		Field Staff and Band, 5th U. S. Cav. and Detachment 12th U. S. Inf.
	Russell Barracks.	Bvt. Lieut. Col. P. W. STANHOPE, Capt. 12th U. S. Inf.	12th Regiment U. S. Inf.
	Reynold's Barracks.	Capt. H. GARDNER, 44th U. S. Inf.	44th Regiment U. S. Inf.
	POSTS.		
	Fort McHenry, Md.,	Brevet Brig. General H. BROOKS, Col. 4th U. S. Artillery.	Head-quarters and Companies "D," and "I," 4th U. S. Artillery.
	Fort Washington, Md.,	Bvt. Col. JOHN MENDENHALL, Cap. 4th U. S. Art.	Companies "A," and "M," 4th U. S. Artillery.
	Fort Foote, Maryland.	Bvt. Lieut. Colonel M. P. MILLER, Captain 4th U. S. Artillery.	Company "E." 4th U. S. Artillery.

J. ROBERTS, Bvt. Brig. Gen., U. S. A., A. A. A. Gen.

OFFICIAL PAPERS.

HEAD-QUARTERS DEPARTMENT OF WASHINGTON,
WASHINGTON, D. C., October 4, 1867.
SPECIAL ORDERS, No. 170.   (Extract.)

1. Brevet Lieutenant Colonel P. W. STANHOPE, Captain 12th U. S. Infantry, having been assigned to the command of a Battalion of eight (8) Companies of his Regiment by competent authority, will be furnished, under the terms of Paragraph II, General Orders No. 277, War Department, A. G. O., August 8, 1863, with one (1) horse, and the requisite horse equipments, by the Quartermaster Department, to be retained by him during his present assignment.

By command of Brevet Major General W. H. Emory,

J. H. TAYLOR,
Brvt. Lt. Col. P. W. STANHOPE,   Assistant Adjutant General.
Capt. 12th U. S. Inf., Commanding Russell Barracks.
Through Head-Quarters Garrison of Washington.

HEAD-QUARTERS DEPARTMENT OF WASHINGTON,
WASHINGTON, D. C., December 2, 1867.
General U. S. GRANT, Secretary of War,

GENERAL:—I beg leave to refer you to the record of Bvt. Lt. Col. Stanhope, Captain of 12th U. S. Infantry, and the various testimonials with which he is furnished by his Commanders in the field, which are herewith inclosed, and to recommend that an additional Brevet be conferred on him. He is a very valuable and efficient officer, in the command, at this time, of eight companies of his Regiment, and the proposition to Brevet him at this time, to a Colonelcy, receives great weight, from the fact that one of the Captains of his Regiment, junior to him and now serving under his command, has just received that promotion.

I have the honor to be your obedient servant,

W. H. EMORY,
Bvt. Maj. Genl. Comdg.

HEAD-QUARTERS DEPARTMENT OF WASHINGTON,
WASHINGTON, D. C., December 27, 1867.
SPECIAL ORDERS, No. 220.   (Extract.)

II. A General Court Martial is hereby appointed to convene at Reynold's Barracks, in this city, at 10 o'clock, A. M., on Thursday, January 2, 1868, or as soon thereafter as practicable, for the trial of Brevet Lieutenant Colonel P. W. Stanhope, Captain 12th U. S. Infantry.

DETAIL FOR THE COURT:

Major General James B. Ricketts, U. S. Army;
Brevet Brigadier General H. Brooks, U. S. Army, Colonel 4th Artillery;

Brevet Brigadier General Geo. P. Buell, U. S. Army, Lt. Col. 29th Infantry;
Brevet Colonel J. Mendenhall, U. S. Army. Captain 4th Artillery;
Brevet Lieutenant Colonel F. Beach, U. S. Army, Captain 4th Artillery;
Major Lyman Bissell, 29th U. S. Infantry;
Major Frank H. Larned, U. S. Army:
Brevet Lt. Col. A. J. McNett, U. S. Army, Captain 44th Inf., Judge Advocate.
No other officers than those named can be assembled without manifest injury to the service.

By command of Brevet Major General W. H. Emory.

J. H. TAYLOR,
Assistant Adjutant General.

PLEA IN BAR.

To the first specification of the 1st charge, guilty, except the word "damned," but attach no criminality thereto.

To the 1st charge, not guilty.

To the specification of the 2nd charge, I plead in bar as follows:

The charges preferred against me, are two in number, each in violation of a separate Article of War, differing totally the one from the other, constituting each a separate offense, and each bearing a separate penalty; whereas the act alleged to have been committed is but one.

The specifications under each charge are identical, word for word. The first charge seems to declare a violation of the 6th Article of War. The second charge a violation of the 99th Article of War, while the act alleged to have been committed, as shown in the specification, is the same in both cases.

It is impossible to plead to these unfortunate charges which seem to have been framed under a vague hope that if one would not cover the ground, the other possibly might.

It is necessary for me, before I plead, to know precisely the offenses with which I am charged, and each charge must be one, single, given in express words, and explained by its own distinct and peculiar specifications.

Therefore to the second charge and its specification I plead as above in bar of trial.

P. W. STANHOPE,
Capt. 12th U. S. Inf., Bvt. Lieut. Col. U. S. Army.

PLEA IN DEFENSE.

The Judge Advocate of this Court, in his answer to my plea in bar, charges me with disrespect to the General Commanding.

May it please the Court, the charge is absurd. That it is so, I propose to show by the tenor of my defense.

I desire, first, to state that my plea in bar of trial was no disrespect toward the Major General Commanding the Department. No officer can have a greater respect than I entertain for him.

My plea in bar was made because it was necessary for me to know with what offense I was charged; under what Article of War I was arraigned.

The additional charge, of the Judge Advocate of this Court, I deny; and, as I said before, my denial will be sustained by the tenor of my defense.

The 99th Article of War expressly excludes trials under any case provided for in the preceding 98 Articles of War. The second charge is laid under the 99th Article of War. To that charge I plead not guilty, and to one of these charges, the last, a demurrer.

I am at a loss to know, from the ruling of the Court, from which charge I shall defend myself, a violation of the 6th Article of War, or a violation of the 99th Article of War.

The Court, in my opinion, should have ordered the Judge Advocate to select one of the two charges under which I should have been tried; this plea was made by me and overruled by the Court, but I was made to meet both charges, and specifications, the specifications being identical, word for word.

At my own table I made use of part of the language set forth in the specification; neither Lieut. Col. Wallace, nor reviewing officer stated in the specifications was present, nor was it addressed to, or intended for them.

Two officers of the 12th Infantry were present, one seated at my side; neither understood my remarks to be addressed to Lieut. Col. Wallace; but one thought they were addressed to him, the other that they were addressed to a 2nd Lieutenant who was seated at the further end of the table, and that Lieut. Col. Wallace was in no way under consideration as the object of this conversation. One of these officers stated to the other that he understood the remarks were intended for him, but was informed by the other that they were intended for 2nd Lieutenant, David G. Craigie, and no one else.

This 2nd Lieut. David G. Craigie, 12th Infantry, reported this conversation to Lieut. Col. Wallace, and, upon his report, action was taken!

My remarks were so vague that the officers seated near me did not understand them to be at all a reflection on Lieut. Col. Wallace, but to be applicable, one to himself the other to Lieut. Craigie; this fact I would have shown had I been allowed to do so, and am fully prepared to show it by witnesses.

How, then, can these remarks, *made by me, at my private table;* so vague that one officer sitting near me did not consider applicable to Lieut. Col. Wallace, be considered in the light of the charge preferred against me? "Comtemptuous and disrespectful conduct, conduct to the prejudice of good order and Military discipline."

On the contrary, my expressions were a compliment to the reviewing officer; inasmuch as they were simply a relation of the truth and facts in his case.

The truth is the truth; and expression of it cannot be regarded as dereliction in any officer, or any case.

In this case I simply expressed the truth, it was a statement of an historical fact, and any historical fact I have a right to express now, though it be about General Grant himself or General Townsend, the able Adjutant General of our Army, who did as much in the Cabinet as perhaps General Grant did in the field.

What discredit, then attaches to Lieut. Col. Wallace for assisting General Townsend, and how, then, can a simple relation of recorded facts which is all that is alleged against me, and which I acknowledge to have made, be construed into a military offense?

When Lieut Col. Wallace, under orders from his superiors in authority, was unfortunately kept from his proper position in the field and filled a place, which his long experience fitted him for, and which no other available officer could fill at that time, I think, showed great moral courage in accepting this position instead of commanding men in the field!

My remarks said at the table, not in any way official, *not supposed to be reportable*, though I have no objection to the report, simply stated *a fact:* how can the simple statement of it be construed into disrespect, or contempt, when, as I have shown above, the statement was a credit to the officer?

Thucydides, (3rd Book,) truly says: "a man is not a soldier until he is willing to face the sneers of his countrymen because he is ordered from the field of battle to serve his country with his pen, and the exercise of his administrative abilities."

He faces the sneers of his countrymen, because he has abandoned the field by order, but does not leave the field of battle from his own free will!

He leaves the field of battle from a superior courage: that courage which alone enables him to meet the sneers of his countrymen; and whilst, if unchecked, would carry him through battery after battery of the enemy.

This courage Lieut. Col. Wallace has shown that he possessed.

How, then, can a statement of this fact, *so honorable to him*, by an officer who simply made this statement, be considered as a slur on Lieut. Col. Wallace instead of praise of his conduct?

This conversation was held at a private mess-table. The officer who reported it, 2nd *Lieut. David G. Craigie, took notes of it,* and to my knowledge, made an official report of the same to Lieut. Col. Wallace!

This report could only have been given to Lieut. Col. Wallace by a spy on the private conversation of officers, held in their private quarters and at their private tables.

Right or wrong as I may be, can this Court suppose, or will they support a private espionage on the conversations of officers held in their private rooms?

Can we not express our opinions, as officers of the Army, about things which occur, without being subjected to a Court Marshal, though such expression may be about a superior officer?

Are we not allowed a free expression of opinions in our private quarters, as citizens of the United States, for all officers are citizens?

We are called upon by the War Department to study our profession; in that pursuit we are called upon to decide between the bad and the good; in every school for Artillery, Cavalry and Infantry, officers of the Army are called upon continually to express their opinions of the great Masters of War.

Some officers are eminent for gallantry in the field. Other officers, equally gallant, are compelled by proper authority to fight the battles of their country with the pen.

Lieutenant Colonel Wallace was desirous of taking active service in the field, that I acknowledge, but he was prevented from pursuing the bent of his desire by orders from superior authority. I think, of course, that Lieutenant Colonel Wallace did right in obeying these orders from superior authority, and my statement at the breakfast-table, in private conversation, was simply a statement of the facts in the case; a compliment rather than a slur to the reviewing officer.

Very Respectfully your obedient servant,

P. W. STANHOPE,
Capt. 12th Inft., Bvt. Lieut. Col., U. S. A.

G. C. M.

Brevet Lieutenant Colonel PHILIP W. STANHOPE, U. S. Army, Captain, 12th Infantry.

HEAD-QUARTERS DEPARTMENT OF WASHINGTON,

WASHINGTON, D. C., January 9, 1868.

GENERAL ORDERS, NO. 3.

1. Before a General Court Martial, of which Major General James B. Ricketts, U. S. Army, is President, convened at Reynold's Barracks, in this city, by virtue of Special Orders, No. 220, dated Head-quarters Department of Washington, Washington, D. C., December 27, 1867, was arraigned and tried:—

Brevet Lieutenant Colonel PHILIP W. STANHOPE, U. S. Army, Captain, 12th Infantry, upon the following charges and specifications:

CHARGE 1st.—"Contemptuous and disrespectful conduct towards his commanding officer."

Specification.—"In this; that he, Brevet Lieutenant Colonel Philip W. Stanhope, U. S. Army, Captain in the 12th Infantry, and at the time commanding officer of Russell Barracks, Washington, D. C., did say in the officers mess-room at said barracks, in the presence and hearing of a number of officers of the Army, citizens and servants—retainers of the camp—'I will have the whole proceedings of that Regimental Court published in pamphlet form and send a copy to every damned officer in the army; accompanied with a biographical sketch of all the parties concerned, commencing with the reviewing officer, illustrated, showing him, while the war was raging, mounted on a stool, fighting furiously with a quill,' or words to that effect; the said reviewing officer, Lieutenant Colonel George W. Wallace, 12th Infantry, being his regimental commander, This at Russell Barracks, Washington, D. C., on or about the 16th day of December, 1867."

CHARGE 2nd.—"Conduct to the prejudice of good order and military discipline."

Specification.—"In this; that he, Brevet Lieutenant Colonel PHILIP W. STANHOPE, U. S. Army, Captain in the 12th Infantry, and at the time commanding officer of Russell Barracks, Washington, D. C., did say in the officers' mess-room, in the presence and hearing of a number of the officers of the army, citizens and servants—retainers of the camp,—'I will have the whole proceedings of that Regimental Court published in pamphlet form and send a copy to every damned officer in the army, accompanied with a biographical sketch of all the parties concerned, commencing with the reviewing officer, showing him, while the war was raging, mounted on a stool, fighting furiously with a quill,' or words to that effect; the said reviewing officer, Lieutenant Colonel George W. Wallace, 12th Infantry, being his regimental commander. This at Russell Barracks, Washington, D. C., on or about the 16th day of December, 1867."

PLEA: To the Specification to 1st Charge.   "Guilty, except the word 'damned,' but attach no criminality thereto."

To the 1st CHARGE,   "Not Guilty,"
To the Specification to 2nd Charge,   "Guilty, except the word 'damned,' but attach no criminality thereto."
To the 2nd CHARGE,   "Not Guilty."

FINDING: Of the Specification to 1st Charge,   "Guilty except the word 'damned,' and of this excepted word *not* guilty;"
Of the 1st CHARGE,   "Guilty;"
Of the Specification to 2nd Charge,   "Guilty except the word 'damned,' and of this excepted word *not* guilty;"
Of the 2nd CHARGE,   "Guilty."

"And the Court does, therefore, sentence him, Brevet Lieutenant Colonel Philip W. Stanhope, U. S. Army, Captain, 12th U. S. Infantry, to be suspended from rank, pay proper and command for the period of four (4) months, and to be confined to the limits of his post or station for the same period."

II. The proceedings, findings and sentence in the foregoing case of Brevet Lieutenant Col. Philip W. Stanhope, U. S. Army, Captain, 12th Infantry, are approved and confirmed. The sentence will be carried into effect, except so much of it as directs the stoppage of pay proper for four (4) months,—which is hereby *remitted*.

III. The General Court Martial, convened by virtue of Special Orders, No. 220,

December 27, 1867, from these Head-Quarters, of which Major General James B. Ricketts, U. S. Army, is President, is hereby dissolved.

By command of Brevet Major General W. H. Emory,

J. H. TAYLOR,
Assistant Adjutant General.

NOTE.—Subsequently an order from same Head-Quarters directed Col. Stanhope to proceed to his home and remain there for the four months, practically giving him a leave of absence for that period, without loss of pay or emoluments. The inference is that the military authorities did not consider his crime very heinous, or this leave could not have been granted to him.

G. C. M. O.
Brevet Lieutenant Colonel P. W. STANHOPE, Captain, 12th U. S. Infantry.

HEAD-QUARTERS, DEPARTMENT OF WASHINGTON,
WASHINGTON, D. C., June 27, 1868.

GENERAL ORDERS, No. 37.

1. Before a General Court Martial which convened at Reynold's Barracks in this city, pursuant to Special Orders No. 94, from these Head-Quarters, dated June 13, 1868, and of which Brevet Major General William H. French, Lieutenant Colonel, 2nd U. S. Artillery, is President, was arraigned and tried:—

Brevet Lieutenant Colonel P. W. STANHOPE, Captain, 12th U. S. Infantry, upon the following charge and specification:

CHARGE—"Disobedience of orders."

Specification—"In this; that he, Captain P. W. STANHOPE, 12th Infantry, Brevet Lieutenant Colonel, U. S. A., did, in violation of orders—of which the following is a copy, viz.,

HEAD-QUARTERS, 12TH U. S. INFANTRY,
Russell Barracks, Washington, D. C., December 20, 1867.

REGIMENTAL ORDERS, No. 175.   (Extract.)

1. Hereafter, when officers in command of detachments believe the welfare of their commands demands the transfer of officers to command companies temporarily, (save and except on parades and drills where companies are without a commissioned officer,) application must be submitted to these head-quarters, for the action of the regimental commander.

By order of Lieutenant Colonel Wallace,

D. J. CRAGIE,
2nd Lieut. 12th Inft., Bvt. Capt., U. S. A.,
Adjutant.

—wrongfully issue the following order, viz.,

HEAD-QUARTERS, RUSSELL BARRACKS,
Washington, D. C., May 22, 1868.

ORDERS, No. 78.   (Extract.)

2. First Lieutenant J. H. MAY, 12th Infantry, Brevet Captain U. S. A., is hereby relieved from duty with Company E, 12th Infantry, and temporarily attached to Company H, 12th Infantry. He will receipt to 2nd Lieutenant James Halloran, 12th Infantry, for all company property, company fund and company fund books.

3. Second Lieutenant James Halloran, Company H, 12th Infantry, will turn over all public property of Company H, 12th Infantry, together with the company fund and company fund books, to 1st Lieutenant J. H. May, 12th Infantry, Brevet Captain U. S. A., taking proper receipts for the same.

By order of Brevet Lieutenant Colonel Stanhope,

J. H. HURST,
2nd Lieut., 12th U. S. Infantry,
Post Adjutant.

"This at Russell Barracks, Washington, D. C., on or about May 22, 1868."

To which charge and specification the accused, Brevet Lieutenant Colonel P. W. STANHOPE, Captain, 12th U. S. Infantry, pleaded

"Not guilty."

"The court * * * having maturely considered the evidence adduced, finds the accused, Brevet Lieutenant Colonel P. W. Stanhope, Captain, 12th U. S. Infantry, as follows:

Of the Specification,—The Court finds the facts set forth in the specification to the charge of 'disobedience of orders,' but as no criminal intent is shown in the evidence, and Post Orders No. 78 appearing to have been issued for the good of the service and without previous knowledge of the existence of Regimental Orders No. 175, it attaches no criminality thereto;

Of the CHARGE,— Not guilty.

"And the Court does, therefore, *acquit* him, Brevet Lieutenant Colonel P. W. Stanhope, Captain, 12th U. S. Infantry."

2. The proceedings, findings, and *acquittal* of the accused, in the foregoing case of Brevet Lieutenant Colonel P. W Stanhope, Captain, 12th U. S. Infantry, are approved He will be released from arrest, and resume his sword.

By command of Brevet Major General W. H. Emory,

J. H. TAYLOR,
Assistant Adjutant General.

OFFICIAL PAPERS.

SAN FRANCISCO, January 31, 1870.

Col. P. W. STANHOPE,

DEAR COLONEL:—In a conversation with General Ord, a few days since, he authorized me to inform you that he would have you assigned to a post where you could have the benefit of your rank, as soon as it could be done. When I spoke to him last summer, after returning from your post, he thought he would assign you to Camp Bidwell, but circumstances made it necessary to send a Cavalry Company there, and this, I suppose, determined him not to change you. I would suggest your addressing him an official communication on the subject, to reach him about two months hence, which will be about the time he will return from Arizona.

I am confident that General Ord is disposed to give officers the benefit of their rank, especially when they are known to be efficient, and hoping you will receive the benefit of yours, I remain, Truly yours, ROGER JONES.

HEAD-QUARTERS OF THE ARMY.
ADJUTANT GENERAL'S OFFICE. WASHINGTON, February 5, 1870.

GENERAL ORDERS, No. 15.

1. Under the provisions of the Act approved January 21, 1870, (General Orders No. 9,) all retired officers who have been assigned to duty will be considered as relieved from such assignment on the 21st instant, and will proceed to such homes as they may elect.

2. Retired officers detailed as Professors at Colleges (under the act of July 28, 1866, section 26,) will be considered as relieved from the detail, but they are at liberty to remain at the Colleges, if they desire, under any private arrangement with the authorities thereof.

3. It is understood that retired officers may enter upon any private business; that they have a right to change their place of residence, or travel at their own pleasure, without further authority, except to leave the United States to go beyond sea (Paragraph 183, Regulations of 1863;) and that, unless specially exempted, they should report their address monthly to the Adjutant General.

4. In thus performing a duty which the law imposes, the Secretary of War and General of the Army take occasion to express their regret that, in the natural course of things, the long continuance of most faithful devotion to duty on the part of the officers concerned must at last terminate. Doubtless in most, if not in all cases, a respite from unceasing toil and responsibility will be grateful, if not necessary, coming as it does in this involuntary form, and without a possibility of implied reproach. The best wishes of the Government for their future comfort and happiness follow these veterans, and those who have preceded them in retirement from all service, to the homes of their choice. By command of General Sherman,

E. D. TOWNSEND,
Adjutant General.

Major STANHOPE, U. S. A., (Relieved.) Through A. C. and P. Branch.

OFFICIAL PAPERS.

Washington, D. C., March 26, 1870.

Dear Captain:—Yours of March 13th is just received. I have enclosed it to the Secretary of the Interior and have endorsed you to him as every way worthy of his confidence.
Very Truly Yours,
J. A. GARFIELD.

Capt. P. W. Stanhope,
Camp Gaston, California.

Gold Bluffs, California, May 4, 1870.

Col. P. W. Stanhope,
Camp Gaston, California.

Sir:—Yours of April 25, came to hand in due time, and I hasten to reply to it. It will be conferring a pleasure if I can in any manner remunerate you for past assistance and services.

At present I have not time to see all the persons whom you so ably saved from immediate death and destruction of property by your prompt and decisive action; but if it is necessary I will write out a statement of the facts at that time and have them to sign it, and, if called upon, corroborate our signatures with our oaths.

If you should need me, or all hands, or a statement, at Hoopah, send word; we will assist you to the best of our abilities, for we are under lasting obligations to you.

Respectfully Yours,
JOHN SANDRIDGE.

Copy of Endorsement on statements of disqualifications in the case of Captain Ph'lip W. Stanhope, 12th Infantry, forwarded by Colonel O. B. Wilcox, 12th Inft.

HEAD-QUARTERS DEPARTMENT OF CALIFORNIA,
San Francisco, Cal., September 15, 1870.

Respectfully returned for reconsideration. From the action at Washington in other cases, it is probable this case would be sent before the Examining Board, and the whole matter should be carefully prepared before hand. Statements and vague accounts of enlisted men, unsupported by 'evidence of unprejudiced persons would not suffice.

By command of General Ord.

SAMUEL BRECK,
Asst. Adjt. Genl.

Colonel O. B. Wilcox, acknowledges receipt of a telegram from A. G. O., October 25, 1870, submits a list of officers not serving in this Department, but who are in the Division of the Pacific, and recommends their transfer to the list of Supernumeraries.

[Copy of Endorsement thereon.]
HEAD-QUARTERS DEPARTMENT OF CALIFORNIA,
SAN FRANCISCO, October 31, 1870.

Respectfully forwarded. These officers are not serving in my Department. Captain Stanhope did so serve up to and after the term at which I was called on for the names of officers who might probably be examined under the recent law, as unfit or unable to serve. I consider him a good officer; his war-record and wounds show great gallantry in the field.

E. O. C. ORD,
Brig., and Bvt. Major Gen. Comd.

Samuel Breck, A. A. G.

Colonel O. B. Wilcox, 12th Infantry forwards papers in Captain Stanhope's case.
[Endorsement thereof.]
HEAD-QUARTERS DEPARTMENT OF CALIFORNIA,
SAN FRANCISCO, November 8, 1870.

Respectfully forwarded. Case of Captain P. W. Stanhope, Brevet Lieutenant Colonel. General Wilcox forwards papers to substantiate recommendation. This officer's case with part of these papers, came before me some time since, and after examining the accounts of Company tailor and laundress, I returned the papers to General Wilcox, who then did not consider the case one which under the law called for action, other officers corroborated Captain Stanhope's statement and the officers named by General Wilcox, as witnesses, who are serving in this Department, are in my opinion, after investigation, governed more by feeling, than a desire to benefit the service. There is at the same time, so much alleged against this officer, that I think in justice to all concerned, his case should be brought before the Board authorized to examine officers, whose alleged unfitness may be due to other causes than injuries received in service. As I before stated, he has been wounded and has a good war-record.

Samuel Breck, A. A. G.

E. O. C. ORD,
Brig., and Bvt. Maj. Gen. Comdg.

I certify that the foregoing are true copies from the files of the Adjutant General's office, Head-Quarters Department of California.

HUGH S. BROWN,
1st Lieut., 12th Inft., A. D. C.

NOTE:—The papers were sent on to Washington, by Colonel Wilcox, without his allowing me a defense, or to be heard, in fact it is stated that he delayed final report until it was impossible for me to have had time to defeat his purpose. I was credibly informed, after my muster out that he had announced it to have been his purpose to delay until it would be too late for me to act. Comment on such an act is quite unnecessary, because none knew better than he, the utter falsity of the statements and the contemptible animus of the conspirators—and that he himself had in my presence questioned the sanity of the leader of the disreputable gang.

SAN FRANCISCO, November 9, 1870.

Col. P. W. STANHOPE,
   Fort Yuma,

DEAR FRIEND:—With pleasure I acknowledge your letter of the 3rd, ultimo, and am glad to hear of your safe arrival at your future home for a time at least. I trust that you will find it a more pleasant one to yourself than Camp Gaston, at least where you are now, you are freed from petty jealousies and annoyances.

I have collected your Pay Roll for October, and sold Greenbacks at 90 cents, leaving a balance of $48.50, in coin which is credited on your note. If I can possibly get away during this winter, I shall pay you a visit.

Excuse this short epistle. Next time more.

        Remain your friend,
          J. GREENEBAUM.

ALCATRAZ ISLAND, CAL., January 10, 1871.

Brigadier General E. O. C. ORD,
 Commanding Department of California,
   San Francisco, Cal.

DEAR SIR:—Knowing your kindly feeling toward Captain Philip W. Stanhope, late 12th Infantry, and Brevet Lieutenant Colonel, U. S. A., I take the liberty of saying a few words in his behalf, with the hope that something may yet be done to right, what I cannot help but consider a great though unintentional wrong done him by the provision of General Orders No. 1, Head-Quarters of the Army, Washington, D. C., January 2, 1871.

My acquaintance with Captain Stanhope commenced in 1862, and I saw considerable of him during the Peninsula Campaign of the Army of the Potomac, and always found him a high toned, pleasant gentleman and officer, with the reputation of being an excellent soldier.

Of Captain Stanhope's moral character, or the reports sent to Washington that caused his discharge from the Army, I know nothing, but if they are no more reliable, than the one so diligently circulated some time since, that he had deserted and failed to support his wife, I should want to give them a very thorough investigation before believing any part thereof, as this report has been proven to me to be utterly false, by letters from Mrs. Stanhope to the Captain, several of which I have seen, in which she speaks in the most affectionate manner, and acknowledges the receipt of different sums of money, in all fully equal to half of his salary.

During the battles of "Mechanicsville" and "Gaines' Mill" Major (now Colonel) H. B. Clitz, was in command of the 12th Infantry, and Stanhope the Senior Captain unwounded. In the latter fight Clitz was very seriously wounded; Captain Stanhope took command, but in a short time he too was wounded, and left upon the field for dead, where he remained until the following day, when he was removed by the Rebels to Richmond, and after a long time, lingering between life and death, he so far recovered as to be exchanged, and again (as I am led to believe though I know nothing of it personally) did good service in the Western Army, and in the Army of the Potomac.

Although Captain Stanhope so far recovered as to perform duty, he never has been, or can be, a sound man, and is, in my opinion, unfit for active service, and should have been retired; one of his arms having been so badly shattered, that it is almost useless, while he suffers almost continually from the effects of his wound, causing paralysis in his side.

If under the circumstances Captain Stanhope's temper is uneven, or he should speak harshly to officers or enlisted men, I think he might often be excused, for he has at least earned the right to be eccentric. I feel myself more particularly called upon to speak in behalf of Captain Stanhope, because at the time the Court-Martial was ordered at Camp Gaston, California, for his trial, on charges perferred by Major Mizner, 12th Infantry, it was owing I believe to my advice, that he decided to let the matter rest after these charges were withdrawn, and this after I had seen official papers sufficient to satisfy me that had he been tried, not one of the allegations against him could have been sustained, and that he would have been honorably acquitted by the Court.

Hoping that something may yet be done for an officer, who, I think, should be retired on the full rank of the command he held when he fell on the field of battle,

I am very respectfully your obedient servant,

J. M. ROBERTSON,
Captain 2nd Artillery, Bvt. Brig. Gen., U. S. Army.

FORT YUMA, CAL., February 11, 1871.

MY DEAR COLONEL:—I take this liberty before parting with you of expressing my many thanks for the uniform courtesy you have extended to me, as a Commanding officer, and gentleman.

Our association, though brief, has been marked throughout with a pleasantness which I cannot do you a greater honor than to wish it may follow you through all your after relations in life.

I am, Colonel, most respectfully your obedient servant,

JOHN J. CLAGUE,
2nd Lieut., 12th Inf.

To Col. P. W. STANHOPE.

ARIZONA CITY, February 11, 1871.

DEAR SIR:—This will be presented to you by Colonel P. W. Stanhope, 12th U. S. Infantry, who has been stationed at Fort Yuma for several months past, relieving Major Parker of the command.

He goes to Washington regarding his having been mustered out by late orders, or congressional action, and says it has been done entirely through personal malice of certain officers, who took advantage of their position to injure him. He desires to re-open the case and have justice done him and I take the liberty of asking you to work in concert with his other influential friends to the end that full justice be done. Since my acquaintance with him I can testify to his good habits, being entirely temperate, &c., &c. I have the honor to remain, Yours respectfully,

J. M. BARNY.

Hon. R. C. McCORMICK,
Washington, D. C.

HEAD-QUARTERS DEPARTMENT OF CALIFORNIA,
SAN FRANCISCO, March 5, 1871.

Gen. E. D. TOWNSEND, Adjutant General,

SIR:—I have the honor to enclose, per hand of applicant, copies of letters from Bvt. Brig. Gen. Robertson, and Ast. Surgeon Bentley, U. S. A., also copies of my endorsements on the allegations, *vs.* Captain P. W. Stanhope late of 12th Infantry.

I still think his case was prejudiced by personal feelings on the part of the officers who originated the charge, and that Captain Stanhope should at least be heard in his defense.

I came to the conclusion after a personal investigation (into similar charges) at the Post of Captain Stanhope, and while a guest in the house of Major Mizner his prosecutor. I am, sir, respectfully your obedient servant,

E. O. C. ORD,
Brig. Gen. Comdg.

POINT SAN JOSE, CAL., March 6, 1871.

Brig. Gen. E. O. C. ORD,
Commanding Dept. of California,

GENERAL:—I have the honor to state that I was Post Surgeon at Russell Barracks, Washington, D. C., from the spring of 1866, until the post was broken up in 1869. During this period Bvt. Lieut. Col. P. W. Stanhope, U. S. A., was commanding officer for nearly two years. My relations with him officially and socially, from my present recollection, were always of the most amiable and pleasant character. I knew Col. Stanhope at Libby Prison, Richmond, Va., in 1862. I found him suffering from gun-shot wound of the elbow joint, from the effects of which he nearly lost his life. At Russell Barracks he was afterwards under my professional care. He suffered extremely from piles. The liver, kidneys, and bowels were at times affected, the result of miasma to which he had been exposed during the war.

Very respectfully your obedient servant,
EDWIN BENTLEY,
Capt. and Asst., Surgeon, Post Surgeon.

DRUM BARRCKS, CALIFORNIA, March 9, 1871.

P. W. STANHOPE,

MY DEAR SIR:—In reply to your letter of the 6th, I take pleasure in saying that I inspected the post of which you had commanded last October, and found it all that could be desired and if this statement can be of any service to you I should be very glad to know it, and am, Very truly and respectfully,

GEORGE STONEMAN,
Col. Comdg. Dept., of Arizona.

PRESIDIO OF SAN FRANCISCO, March 13, 1871.

CAPTAIN P. W. STANHOPE,
Cincinnati, O.

DEAR SIR:—I regret not seeing you before you left this Coast to express my sincere regards for your misfortune. I do feel when the United States loses your service as a U. S. Officer, that the Country is deprived of one of its most faithful subjects. I know you have many enemies, but they are of a class of men who are ever ready to shirk their duty. I have served with you and under you and take pleasure in recalling the many happy moments. We never had any trouble because we both did our duty, and I have always said, and you are at liberty to use my name in saying, that an officer who is willing to do his duty will ever find it pleasant to serve under you. Truly yours,

J. H. LORD,
Regimental Quarter-Master, 2nd Art.

FORT HALL, IDAHO, April 9, 1871.

DEAR COLONEL:—Replying to your note of March 25, I deem it but a simple act of justice to say, that during my period of service under your command I was treated with every courtesy and kindness both socially and officially on all occasions.

Very truly yours,
J. E. PUTNAM,
Captain 12th Infantry.

Colonel P. W. STANHOPE,
Cincinnati, Ohio.

OFFICIAL PAPERS.

FORT YUMA, CALIFORNIA, May 17, 1871.

P. W. STANHOPE, Late Captain,
U. S. 12th Infantry.

SIR:—My acquaintance with you first began in the month of September, 1866, at Washington City, D. C., when you were exercising the command of the 1st Battalion, 12th Infantry and Camp Augur, since which time, up to the date of your muster out of service, you had several important commands, the last being that of this post.

During all of the time we were together on duty in Washington City you had your friends as well as enemies. For myself, individually, I never had any cause of complaint in doing duty under you and believe others could perform their duties under you without complaint, as I found you to be a thorough-going soldier and prone to have others do their duty. Very respectfully your obedient servant,

JOHN L. VIVEN.
1st Lieut. 12th Inft., Bvt. Capt., U. S. A., Late R. Q. M., and Act. Adjt.

CAMP INDEPENDENCE, CALIFORNIA, May 19, 1871.

DEAR COLONEL:—In reply to your letter of March 27, 1871, it is with pleasure that I can state that I served under your command, from August, 1866 to December, 1867; the last six months as your Adjutant, when you commanded at Russell Barracks, Washington, D. C., and during all of that time our relations were of the very pleasantest. At no time did I find any difficulty in maintaining such relations. I can freely say that I have never served with a more pleasant Commanding Officer.

With much respect, your obedient servant,
W. E. DOVE,
1st Lieut. 12th Inft.

SAN DIEGO, CALIFORNIA.

DEAR COLONEL:—We reached here all right, this morning, but nearly froze during the two nights of the trip. Met the other detachment near New River. I can't find out any thing about that carbine here, and I think the best way will be to charge it to Crooks at once. Reed and myself both desire to thank you again for your kindness to us. Captain Craig, also, sends his compliments. Morrow, Paymaster, is expected in to-morrow's steamer. No other news that I can learn.

Yours truly,
C. E. KILBOURNE,
2nd Lieut. 2nd Arty.

OFFICIAL PAPERS.

WASHINGTON, D. C., November 25, 1871.

Capt. P. W. STANHOPE,
    Springfield, Ohio.

DEAR SIR:—Yours of the 22nd inst. is received. I scarcely know what course to take to serve you, in your present situation. The application, made by me last year, was refused by the Secretary of War, and the case was laid before the President, bringing no different result.

Perhaps the course which you now suggest, being different in form, can result successfully. You had better consult with Mr. Shellabarger, before he leaves home, and probably you had better make a special application, such as you speak of, to be appointed as 2nd Lieutenant for the purpose of going before the Retiring Board. I shall cheerfully do all I can for you, though success appears doubtful in view of the decision already made. Very truly yours,

J. A. GARFIELD.

DEPARTMENT OF THE INTERIOR, PENSION OFFICE,
WASHINGTON, D. C., January 6, 1875.

SIR:—You are hereby notified that your claim for pension, No. 126,752, has been allowed at $20.00 per month, commencing 7th of October, 1874, payable at the Pension Agency in Cincinnati, Ohio.

Your pension certificate has been issued and sent to the Pension Agent at the same place, who will forward to you, upon receipt thereof, and quarterly thereafter, proper vouchers for payment thereupon. The note indorsed upon said vouchers will explain when and how they shall be executed by you, and how the payment thereupon will be made.

The fee to be paid your attorney for the prosecution of your claim is $10.00 and no more, and the same will be deducted from first payment by Pension Agent.

J. H. BAKER,
Commissioner.

To PHILIP W. STANHOPE.

HEAD-QUARTERS OF THE ARMY, ADJUTANT GENERAL'S OFFICE,
WASHINGTON, February 27, 1877.

Captain P. W. STANHOPE,
    Late of the 12th Infantry,
        Care of General Charles Ewing,
            Washington, D. C.

SIR:—Referring to your letter of the 16th instant, requesting a copy of the report which led to your muster out of service, you are respectfully informed that under date of March 23, 1869, your regimental commander reported you as a proper subject to be placed on awaiting orders; that you were "a mischievous and insubordinate officer," and had been tried and found guilty by a General Court-Martial of contemptuous and disrespectful conduct to your commanding officer, &c. In 1870 he again reported you as unfit for the proper discharge of your duties; that you were ungentlemanly and unofficer-like in your conduct, that you were *then* detached from your company on account of difficulties with your Post Commander, who had preferred charges and specifications against you; that you were indebted to the company tailor and laundress, and, further, that you had passed yourself "as an unmarried man, to the injury of a young lady in Washington," that you made "false reports," &c.

The foregoing record and reports led to your transfer to the list of supernumeraries, and honorable discharge, under Section 12, Act of July 15, 1870, in pursuance of the plan adopted by the General of the Army and Secretary of War to retain in service, as far as possible, only those officers whose records were clear.

Very respectfully your obedient servant,
E. D. TOWNSEND,
Adjutant General.

NOTE:—After some six years endeavor to ascertain cause for this muster out this reply was received. Now, the officer who encumbered my record with Courts-Martial did so designedly, and for the express purpose of being able to cite these very charges to my injury in the future. The letters of Gen. Robertson to Gen. Ord, and the latter's indorsements, show conclusively what Mizner's withdrawn charges amounted to. In these, had they been tried, all the questions cited by the Adjutant General's letter above would have been disposed of by the Court and very much to the confusion of said Mizner; and probably would have led to his punishment for presuming to impose upon the service such falsehoods.

The above letter is based on the reports emanating from and duly fostered and nursed by Wallace and Mizner. My record as a soldier and gentleman, *with* soldiers and gentleman is not comparable to theirs. I am Pharisee enough to "thank God I am not like" either of these or "other men" of their class.

MADISON BARRACKS,
SACKET'S HARBOR, N. Y., December 12, 1877.

MY DEAR STANHOPE:—I have just received your letter of the 4th and am glad to learn that you have some prospects of redress. If you think I can be of any service to you, and get me ordered to Washington, I shall come with a great deal of pleasure. Mrs. Robertson desires to be remembered. Yours truly,
J. M. ROBERTSON.
Brevet Brigadier General.

PROVIDENCE, R. I., January 4, 1878.

MY DEAR COLONEL:—You may rely upon my support of your interests. What the committee will do I cannot say.

I will upon my return to Washington do what I can in the matter. With best regards I remain,
Very truly yours,
A. E. BURNSIDE.

To COL. STANHOPE.

HOUSE OF REPRESENTATIVES,
WASHINGTON, D. C., June 5, 1878.

Capt. P. W. STANHOPE,

MY DEAR SIR:—It will give me great pleasure to comply with your request contained in yours of the 3rd instant.

I will, to-day, see some of the members of the Military Committee of the Senate and urge prompt action on your bill, and of course favorable action.

Yours most truly,
J. WARREN KEIFER.

WASHINGTON, D. C., April 19, 1879.

MY DEAR MAJOR:—Your nomination as Major went to the Senate yesterday. I will press an early confirmation. Perhaps you had better write to General Burnside, and other of your friends, if you feel like it, although I think it is hardly necessary. I congratulate you sincerely. Merit will win in the end; the chickens come home to roost to evil doers. I think I know your history well and shall be able to set you all right if attempts are made to malign you in any way. I don't think it will be necessary for me to vindicate you before the Secretary of War, as suggested in your letter received this morning, but, should it become necessary, I will not be slack in discharge of my duty to a faithful and brave officer, that you may rely on.

This morning finds me in the midst of several engagements.

Most respectfully,
R. P. LOWE.

UNITED STATES SENATE CHAMBER,
WASHINGTON, D. C., May 4, 1879.

MY DEAR MAJOR:—It is not proper for me to say anything of the nature of the action of the committee until it is made public in the regular way. I may say, however, that I agree with the view you take of your case, and further, that I do not think you are in any danger of a failure of confirmation. It will give me great pleasure to try to hasten it. Very truly your friend,

A. E. BURNSIDE.

To Col. P. W. STANHOPE.

COMMITTEE WAYS AND MEANS, HOUSE OF REPRESENTATIVES,
WASHINGTON, D. C., May 27, 1879.

MY DEAR COLONEL:—Your favor is received. I have regretted that it was not possible to hasten the confirmation of your promotion, but it got entangled in the committee with the others and it was difficult to get a report. Finally, however, the committee reported in favor of yours, but *against* the others. The Senate, nevertheless, confirmed all.

I shall send you a few copies of my speech in the House, and at Tammany Hall, and ask you to send them to your friends. Yours truly,

J. G. CARLISLE.

Col. P. W. STANHOPE.

SHAKOPEE, July 25, 1879.

Col. P. W. STANHOPE,
   Cincinnati,

MY DEAR COLONEL:—Yours of the 2nd inst. received. I should have acknowledged receipt sooner but have been absent from home. I am pleased to learn that you are well and that you have succeeded in being re-instated. The fact is you never should have been mustered out, or dropped from the rolls, but once out you will know how hard it is to get re-instated. I most certainly would be pleased to see you, and hope to have the pleasure of doing so at no distant day. Remember me to Captain Kinney. I am, very truly,

H. B. STRAIT.

PRINTER'S No. 1960.
45th Congress, 2nd Session. H. R. 1901.
IN THE HOUSE OF REPRESENTATIVES,

December 5, 1877.

Read twice, referred to the Committee on Military Affairs, and ordered to be printed.
Mr. Carlisle, by unanimous consent, introduced the following bill:

A BILL

For the relief of Philip W. Stanhope.

Be it enacted by the Senate and House of Representatives of the United States of America in Congress assembled, that Philip W. Stanhope, late captain of the Twelfth United States Infantry and brevet lieutenant-colonel of the United States

Army, having been placed upon the list of supernumeraries, from which he was mustered, under the mistake of groundless charges as the superinducing cause thereof, be, and he is hereby, restored to his proper rank and promotion in the Army, with directions to the Secretary of War, on account of his disabilities incurred in the line of duty, to place him on the retired list, without regard to the limit as to numbers heretofore fixed by law; and that the Secretary of the Treasury, out of any money in the Treasury not otherwise appropriated, shall pay to him his pay and emoluments as if his service had been continuous from the date of his muster-out, less the one year extra pay.

45th Congress, 3rd Session.   SENATE.   Report No. 649.

IN THE SENATE OF THE UNITED STATES.
January 28, 1879.—Ordered to be printed.
Mr. SPENCER, from the Committee on Military Affairs, submitted the following
REPORT:
[To accompany bill H. R. 1901.]

The Committee on Military Affairs, to whom was referred the bill (H. R. 1901) for the relief of Philip W. Stanhope, have had the same under consideration, and submit the following report:

This officer was a captain in the Twelfth United States Infantry, and was placed upon the list of supernumeraries and musterd out under provisions of the act of July 15, 1870. It appears, however, that General Ord, his department commander, and the only officer authorized by said act to make report of officers for muster out, *did not* report him on the list of officers to be made supernumerary and mustered out. Subsequently some charges appear to have been interposed against Captain Stanhope which were absolutely unwarranted and untrue, and in consequence thereof he was mustered out under section 12 of said act, without being accorded the privilege, as provided in said act, of going before the board to meet and disprove them. Had he been permitted thus to meet them, the record attests the fact that they could not have been sustained.

The following is the report of the Committee on Military Affairs of the House of Representatives on this case, which is substantiated by the record, and in the legal conclusions of which your committee agree:

[House report No. 253. Forty-fifth Congress, second session.]

February 27, 1878.—Committed to the Committee of the Whole House and ordered to be printed.

Mr. STRAIT, from the Committee on Military Affairs, submitted the following report (to accompany bill H. R. 1901.)

OFFICIAL PAPERS.

The Committee on Military Affairs, to whom was referred the bill (H. R. 1901) for the relief of Philip W. Stanhope, late captain and brevet lieutenant-colonel United States Army, asking to be restored to his command, and put upon the retired-list for reasons therein stated, beg leave to report:

That they have duly considered the statements made in the petition of Philip W. Stanhope, and the large number of papers, and documents, and proofs accompanying the same, and find the following to be the substantial facts of the case:

That he was appointed captain of the Twelfth United States Infantry on the 14th day of May, 1861; that he served in the field during the entire late war, except the short period he was in Libby Prison, and while he was recovering from severe gun-shot wounds; that he was sober and regular in his habits; a skillful and efficient officer; that he was brevetted twice during the war for gallantry in battle, and left a war record that was as honorable to the service as it was creditable to him.

After the war he continued in the service until the 13th of February, 1871, when he was mustered out under the provisions of an act of Congress passed on the 15th of July, 1870, for reducing the numerical force of the Army, including a corresponding number of officers. The eleventh and twelfth sections of said act prescribed two methods of designating the officers that should be mustered out of the military service.

Under the first of these two sections the General of the Army and the commanding officers of the several military departments were required to report to the Secretary of War a list of officers serving in their respective commands that might be deemed unfit for the proper discharge of their duties from any cause, except for injuries incurred in the line of duty. This list when made out was submitted to a board of five officers, organized by the Secretary of War, on whose recommendation the President was authorized to muster out, &c. Under this method, each officer included in the list was allowed to appear before the board and show cause against it. This last provision of the law carries with it as a necessary incident, as your committee suppose, the right on the part of the officer to be notified if he was put on the list on account of any charges affecting his character as such officer, in order that he should have an opportunity to vindicate himself in case the charges should be unfounded.

Now, your committee find from the evidence that the General and the commanders of the several military departments, and who are supposed to be unprejudiced and well acquainted with the character of their subordinate officers, did not include Captain Stanhope among the unfit officers to be mustered out, and it follows, as we suppose, on the other hand, that they deemed him a proper officer to remain in the service. Indeed, we find among the papers and proofs letters of General Ord, commanding his department, indorsing Captain Stanhope as a worthy officer and having a fine war record, &c.

The second method under the twelfth section authorized the President to transfer officers from the different regiments to the supernumeraries, and from this list to fill any vacancies which might occur in the Army, from any cause, prior to the 1st of

January, 1871, and all that should remain of the list after that date should be mustered out; this was done, including Captain Stanhope, who had been put upon this list under circumstances which, in the opinion of your committee, were illegal and against the true intent of the act of Congress, not to say highly injurious to the reputation of a worthy and good officer.

The committee find from the evidence that this officer was placed upon the supernumerary list in consequence of certain false and malicious charges and representations, secretly made near the close of the period in which the list under the law was to be made, seriously affecting his character as an officer, and of which he was kept in ignorance until about a year ago. It is alleged that these charges were preferred by Lieutenant-Colonel Wallace and Major Mizner, of the twelfth Regiment. The evidence shows that these two officers were very unfriendly and hostile to Captain Stanhope for some unknown cause; that Lieutenant-Colonel Wallace, particulary, had been so for a number of years; that he was oppressive toward the captain, and subjected him to many indignities. The evidence submitted shows that these charges were the occasion of this officer's being placed upon the supernumerary list, without which he would not have been put there and so mustered out. The evidence also disproves these charges, and shows them to be utterly unfounded.

Your committee are inclined to think that where an officer was to be mustered out upon charges affecting his character as an officer, he should have been put upon the list contemplated by the eleventh section so as to give him an opportunity to defend himself. As this was not done, and as the commanding officers of the different departments passed him over and indorsed him as a competent officer to remain in the service, your committee conclude his muster out was illegal, unjust, and without the authority of law; and that there should be some remedy for this great wrong, they would recommend the passage of the amended bill which accompanies this report, and, as amended, they recommend its passage.

The following is a summary of the principal papers on file in this case:

Letters of the Adjutant-General containing a list of the charges which constituted the inducing cause to his (Captain Stanhope's) muster out.

Letters or indorsement of General E. O. C. Ord, dated October 31, 1870, declining to recommend Captain Stanhope for muster out, and closing by saying, "I consider him a good officer; his war record and wounds show great gallantry in the field."

Indorsement of General Ord, dated November 8, 1870, referring to these charges on which Captain Stanhope was mustered out, in which he says, "Other officers corroborated Captain Stanhope's statement, and the officers, named by General Wilcox as witnesses, who are serving in this department, are, in my opinion, after investigation, governed more by feeling than a desire to benefit the service."

Again, March 5, 1871, after Captain Stanhope's muster out, General Ord states in a letter to the Adjutant General, "I still think his case was prejudiced by personal feeling on the part of the officers who originated the charges, and Captain Stanhope should at least be heard in his defense."

OFFICIAL PAPERS.

Letter of Captain J. M. Robertson, 2nd United States Artillery, dated January, 10, 1871, to General E. O. C. Ord, in which, speaking of the high moral character, bravery, gallant service during the late war, and the wounds from which he still suffers, and then of the untruthful reports put in circulation about him, that officer says, "I feel myself more particularly called upon to speak in behalf of Captain Stanhope, because at the time the court-martial was ordered at Camp Gaston, Cal., for his trial on charges preferred by Major Mizner, 12th United States Infantry, it was owing, I believe, to my advice that he decided to let the matter rest; and this after I had seen official papers sufficient to satisfy me that, had he been tried, not one of the allegations against him could have been substantiated, and that he would have been honorably acquitted by the court."

Captain Robertson, it appears, was one of the members of the court-martial detailed in May, 1870, to try Captain Stanhope on these charges, but the charges were withdrawn by the person preferring them when the court was assembled.

Then follow twenty-four certificates of Army officers, all testifying to good character and bravery, which show that he was an exceptionally good officer, and against whom nothing touching his honor could truthfully be said.

It further appears in the record that Captain Stanhope is now receiving pension for *total disability* by reason of wounds received in battle, a fact which does not appear in the House report, no doubt unintentionally omit ed Hence, his retirement, as contemplated by the act, would seem eminently proper as part of the relief sought.

The premises considered, your committee find that Captain Stanhope was a meritorious and honorable officer, and that the brevets received by him for gallantry in action were deserved; that his muster out under attendant circumstances was in conflict with the intendments of the act of July 15, 1870, and that therefore his case is exceptional. Wherefore your committee recommend concurrence of the Senate in the said act, and that it become a law.

[PUBLIC—NO. 78.]
AN ACT FOR THE RELIEF OF PHILIP W. STANHOPE.

Be it enacted by the Senate and House of Representatives of the United States of America in Congress assembled, That Philip W Stanhope, late captain of the 12th United States Infantry and brevet lieutenant-colonel of the United States Army, having been placed upon the list of supernumeraries, from which he was mustered, under the mistake of groundless charges as the superinducing cause thereof, the President of the United States be, and he is hereby, authorized to restore him to his proper, rank and promotion in the Army, with directions to the Secretary of War, on account of his disabilities incurred in the line of duty, to place him on the retired list without regard to the limit as to numbers heretofore fixed by law: *Provided*, That he receive no pay or allowances for the time he was out of service, other than that already received at the time of his muster out: *Provided further*, That he receive no pension while on the retired list.

Approved, March 3, 1879.

U. S. SENATE CHAMBER,
WASHINGTON, D. C., May 23, 1879.

To Major P. W. STANHOPE,
    No. 22 East 3rd Street,
        Cincinnati, Ohio.

You were confirmed to-day. Congratulate you.

A. E. BURNSIDE.

ADJUTANT GENERAL'S OFFICE,
WASHINGTON, May 31, 1879.

SIR:—I forward herewith your Commission of Major of Infantry, your receipt and acceptance of which you will please acknowledge without delay, reporting at the same time your age and residence when appointed, the State where born, and your full name, correctly written. Fill up, subscribe, and return as soon as possible, the accompanying oath, duly and carefully executed.

I am, sir, very respectfully, your obedient servant,

E. D. TOWNSEND,
Adjutant General.

Major PHILIP W. STANHOPE, U. S. Army,
    P. O. Box No 50, Cincinnati, Ohio.

HEAD-QUARTERS OF THE ARMY, ADJUTANT GENERAL'S OFFICE,
WASHINGTON, May 31, 1879.

SPECIAL ORDERS No. 128.   (Extract.)

7. By direction of the President, Philip W. Stanhope, having been appointed a Major in the U. S. Army under authority conferred by the act of March 3, 1879, is

hereby placed on the retired list of the Army in that grade, as of the date of his appointment, May 29, 1879, in conformity with the provisions of said act.

By command of General Sherman,

E. D. TOWNSEND,
Adjutant General.

Official: A. H. Dickenson, Asst. Adj. Gen.

Major STANHOPE, through A. C. and B. Branch, with G. O. 15 of 1870.

In concluding these Official Papers it is proper to note that two have been mislaid and cannot now be found; both are testimonials of the highest character, one from Major General A. E. Burnside, commanding the 9th Army Corps, Army of the Potomac; the other from Brigadier General Joseph B. Hays, commanding the Regular Brigade, 5th Army Corps, same Army.

All the documents show an unbroken line of commendation of myself as a soldier, from every Commanding General under whom I had the honor to serve.

Perhaps it is in order to state that efficient soldiers met with no difficulties, or official discourtesy and outrage, *until after peace was won by them*; then some of them came under the command of those who took no part in the dangers and privations of war or, at the best, such an insignificant part as to have classed them with the non-combatants of the Army of the Union. Under the irritating command of these fierce *peace* soldiers it is not to be wondered at that their want of discretion, and consideration for brave men (only to be acquired in the school of active warfare, and the perils incident thereto) should have resulted in the bad feeling that naturally arose between those having a war-record and those without this claim to consideration and respect.

All brave soldiers respect one another, whether friends or enemies. The true soldier, in time of war, marches to the front (if his proper duty and place call him to command,) and, whatever his orders may be, during the existence of a protracted war, he will, sometimes, be found in the line of battle; there to make manifest his fitness for the commission accorded to him in aid of the defense of his country, and to win a record of which his comrades may be proud, and not ashamed.

Since this is within the option of all regimental officers, whose proper place is at the head of their men in time of war, none may fairly plead a justification for *habitual absence* from the battle field.

Had this principle obtained, *without exception*, in our Armies, many brave and valuable officers would have been secure from unmerited misfortunes and oppression, and the Army itself have been entirely free of one element not soldierly and good.

As it is, the irrepressible conflict, between the combatants and the *non-combatants* of the service, still goes on, whenever the latter come to command the former, and the real war time in the Army is when the most profound peace prevails elsewhere in the Nation.

GEORGE, THE XII–'S.

LINES FOUND IN A FREED-MAN'S BUREAU.

> "He who doth these boots displace
> Must meet Bombastes face to face.
> * * * * *
> Ay, me, what perils do environ
> The man that meddles with cold iron!"
> —BUTLER.

ALMOST A BRIGADIER
OR
GEORGE, THE XIITH ('S)

A WARRIOR OF MANY BATTLES BUT IN NO WAR!
WHOSE MOTTO SHOULD BE

IN BELLUM PACE,—IN PACE BELLUM.

AND

WHOSE EPITAPH SHOULD READ:

"HE LOOKED UPON BATTLE—AFAR OFF!"

TO
THE FOUNDERS OF THE FAME OF
THE TWELFTH UNITED STATES INFANTRY,

1861-5,

This work is respectfully inscribed, with the author's profound respect, affectionate regard, and a sufferer's sympathy.

> "Sic semper," et transitory,
> All such—"military glory!"
> —IBID.

If, when a youth, this warlike soul
  Had dared to win a soldier's glory,
And even fought the Seminole,
  My pen could write a braver story:
    But he was no gunpowder fool-,
    His fort-e is—an office stool.
Again, when orders came to march
  With Taylor, and with Scott to go
To the frontier, and take the starch
  Out of the Dons in Mexico,
    Discretion was his instant scheme—
    He promptly sought an inland stream.

Had he but half the pluck he claims,
  And drawn his sword, and led his men
From the Potomac to the James,
  Instead of drawing his steel—pen!
    And, bravely, each thirtieth day,
    His extra and his fogy pay!
But Seminole, and Mexican,
And Rebel lines, and stockade grim,
Delighted not this—veteran.
  They all were leagues and leagues from him.
    In war he marches to the rear—
    The sound of cannon in his ear!

Our service has one needless shame,
  Some one with rank, but coward soul,
In Peace commands brave men; the same
  As if his deeds were on fame's roll!
    Though never seeing burst of shells,
    Or knowing how gunpowder smells.
But made it study of his life
  Some soft detail in war to get,
And, with his demijohns and wife,
  Worked for promotion and—brevet!
    Keeping his "Register" well filled
    With cheerful notes of Seniors—"killed."

Now, when the fighting is all o'er,
  To take command these fellows come—
(To teach us all the art of war!—
  With dress-parades and majors'-drum,)
    Courts-Martial for the one who dares
    To have a record shaming theirs.
Of course they have forgotten drill,
  And cannot learn the tactics new:
And mix the columns up until
  No mortal can the mess undo:
    Then have to call subordinate
    To "straighten out" and regulate.

They let their angry passions rise,
  Because the knowing rank and file
Look on a soldier with proud eyes,
  And at Bombastes slyly smile.
    Then come the charges, and a court,
    To try the officers who—fought!
"Disobedience—disrespect (?)"
  And all that's in the "99!"
How can the ink-slinger expect
  The veneration of the line?
    A man who slaughters valiant men
    With "ARNOLD's FLUID" and a—pen!

Blood's in his eye—Hector's in sight—
  When he belts on his maiden blade
(All innocent of any fight)
  And sallies forth to—dress-parade.
    Jove's thunders load his eyebrows bent
    As he looks down the line's "present."
And, when he doth toledo draw,
  His face is awful stern and grim;
As if the very gods of war
  Were all concentrate—One—in him;
    And he—Bellona's oriflamme—
    Certain destruction's great I AM!

Splendid the black feathers in his hat,
  (The "white," in PEACE, he does not show!)
Wide, the red sash, round belly fat,
  Bravely the sabre bangs below.
    We see, in him, with bated breath,
    "Bloody murder and sudden death!"
And, when he roars out—"attention!"
  Our fright erects each sep'rate hair;
His voice (a twenty-inched gun)
  Thunders upon the peaceful air—
    We stand on tip-toe (cannoniers)
    Lest the concussion burst our ears!

Sometimes he mounts his "I. C." steed,
  Intent upon battalion drill;
Jomini is nowhere—indeed
  Poor, the first Napoleon's skill;
    And Cæsar, and dark Hannibal?
    He, easy, double-discounts all!
His, the military straddle—
  With trowsers crawling to his knees;
Daylight, plenty, between saddle
  And re-inforced seat of those.
    He is all grace from head to heel,
    And Centaur-like—a sack of meal!

But when he orders, "Double Time!"
And strikes into a small dog trot,
His horsemanship is grand—sublime!
He bounces over ev'ry spot,
From tail of horse, to horse's neck—
A castaway and total wreck!
His uniform looks tempest tost;
His hands seek comfort in the mane;
Now this, now that, wild stirrup's lost
And vaguely toed into again—
His whole demeanor and array
Suggest some desperate foray!

His back describes Hogarth's true line
Of beauty, in acutest curve;
His shoulders, also, this define;
His face lacks dignity and nerve;
His hands in mane and bridle twist—
Harmless the sword slung to his wrist!
Fools know "a hand-saw from a hawk,"—
Wisdom leaves destiny her course;
This man, EXPRESSLY MADE TO WALK,
Must always ride a trotting horse!
George, pedestrian, breaks the rule,
Unless when mounted—on a stool.

Shakespeare, with pen of prophecy,
  Over two centuries ago,
Had George in his foreseeing eye,
  And painted this modern hero—
    When sketching that pot-valiant soul,
    Who drank his courage from the bowl.
To "ancient Bardolph" back we trace
  Our furious rear-guard hero's
Red "hell-fire burning" in his face,
  And lurid pharos for a nose—
    His greatness feeds upon the meat
    In whisky mashes—"sour and sweet."

Yes! "History repeats itself!"
  Our George is also fond of sack—
So fond it laid him on the shelf,
  Whence he shall never stagger back
    To exercise his drunken spleen
    On better men than he has been.
No more Courts-Martial have to wait
  For him to sober up and try
The private who may emulate
  His ruling passion for "red-eye"—
    No more to dock the soldier's pay,
    For getting drunk the COLONEL'S way!

GEORGE THE XII—'S.

O, Justice! hide your head outraged;
 Open your eyes: balance your scales;—
A drunken officer engaged
 In fining lovers of cock-tails!—
  Was ever greater folly seen?
  The Demijohn—*vs.* Canteen!
Our soldiers are most patient here—
 But discipline is very strong;
Else, sometimes, on remote frontier,
 The vicious might resent this wrong.
  Commissioned topers then would get
  Their dues, for bad examples set.

"A prisoner on his parole"—
 So others were, paroled like you;
But Twiggs kept this strategic soul
 From showing Armies how to do;
  But did not keep the braver ones
  From capturing the Rebel guns!
George—a natural quill-driver—
 Has, for all wars, a mortal fear
That drives him to some inland river
 (Some river safe enough in rear);
  There he waits; mustering, writing—
  Anything, to keep from fighting!

There, Sampson (of the cabinets)
Learns to bedevil, with the quill,
The soldiers spared by bayonets
For a deadlier, meaner ill—
    The little tyrannies laid on
    By bravos of the demijohn!
Orders that grind, duties that fret;
Untrue reports on abler men;
These are the wounds that "Martinet"
Stabs into valor—with his pen.
    His little soul jealous with fear
    Of those who read their titles clear!

Sad from Texas he departed,
Saying "the rebel cause was just"—
(This northern man, all southern-hearted,
And ready to betray his trust.)
    He gave, what comforted his soul,
    To rebel Twiggs—cheerful parole.
A pledge nobody deemed sacred,
And void by circumstance and law;
But what his cowardice and hatred
Made his excuse for shirking war.
    And so he to promotion came,
    A crowing rooster—but not "game."

GEORGE THE XII—'S.

Forty years; and not a fight
  Has this white feather ever seen;
Meanwhile brave millions, in their might,
  On countless battle-fields have been
      Fighting at home, fighting abroad—
      And never did HE draw his sword.
Forty years this paper-folder
  Serenely drew his monthly pay;
And should he serve till forty older
  He will contrive to sneak away
      From hostile forces when they shoot,
      And beg for details to recruit.

What Uncle Samuel ought to do—
  If justice is by right inspired,
Is to weed out the coward few;
  Not place them on the list retired!
      The long-serving, wounded, brave
      Only should have this army grave.
No useless, dissipated sot
  Should find this refuge open wide—
His name recorded there to blot
  Those the whole nation reads with pride.
      The martial soldier and the true
      Alone adorn the army blue!

Honor, true justice must contain,
  It can ask for nothing higher—
The blood of every soldier slain
  Cries out against this outrage dire,—
    Cries out for what is just and best;
    An UNCONTAMINATED rest!
And freedom from Department power,
  That all its love of kindred lends
For quick promotion, when the hour
  Draws near to serve relations, friends;
    And musters out the gallant ones,
    To save the cousins, nephews, sons!

This difference may often be
  Between two glories in one sphere—
Great Sherman, marching to the sea!
  George, malingering in the rear.
    One, winning fame and victory,
    One, choosing "blank" in History.
With soldiers this distinction broad
  Is honored and respected still—
All records written with the sword
  Are safe from envy's coward quill!
    Armies win battles only when
    The sword is sharper than the pen!

Never did the Rebellion yield
   Until command was all transferred
From Cabinets unto the field—
    Then, was victory's voice first heard!
      Committees, Editors, and all,
      No longer played the General.
That hour his orders were supreme
   The rebel cause began to wane;
And soon the soldier lived his dream—
   The legions marching home again!
      THEN our ferocious home-guard saw
      'Twas time for HIM to think of war!

He wiped his pen, and, from his blade,
   Festooning cobwebs, and the rust—
Sought for his uniform mislaid.
   Four years of mustering and—dust!
      He got some crippled pensioner
      To polish up—"Excalibur!"
Straightway to Washington he goes—
   To criticise the Great Review,
And talk among the war's heroes
   As if HIS jaw-bone millions slew—
      This—Joshua! that Moon nor Sun
      Waited his battle—lost or won!

Powder, black, democratic drug,
  Will kill—with fine or coarsest grains,
And sends, impartially, the slug
  Or shell, through wise or foolish brains.
    Charged-bayonets, from point to shank,
    Have small respect for any rank!
So, if you wish to save your skin,
  And win promotion (George's way);
Get a detail some office in,
  And draw full commutation pay—
    Command this noble writing school,
    From his own hobby-horse, a stool!

And when you come, to take command
  Of veterans—spared by the war;
Who won their honors—sword in hand,
  In battle-fields you never saw;
    File charges; that will make them think
    True glory lies in pen and ink!
And, if brevets these soldiers wear—
  Offensive to your own career;
Get mad, and very drunk, and swear
  You "should be made a brigadier!"
    The Senate vote was very hard
    On YOUR brevet—my brave Home-Guard!

The Army smiled at your distress—
  In the High Court of Impeachment;—
When Butler made you there confess
  Why you often sought the President—
    An officer, unknown in war,
    BEGGING—for a General's star!!
Did you suppose the fighting men
  Would, really, let you have your way,
And take no care to post up Ben,
  And Senators to vote you—"Nay?"
    "SICK, semper," et transitory,
    All seen "Military Glory!"

From splendid leading to—the worst,
  Brave Clitz to—George of no renown.
White feather for Battalion First?
  Down, eagles of the Twelfth, crawl down!
    Fold up your colors, put them by;
    "Bombastes" hath the victory.
Eyesores, the crowded battle names
  On standards by noblest chrism dim;—
In the red glare of battle flames
  They never floated over him!
    Pray for a war his rage to cool
    And make him hunt another stool.

All honor to the brave that write
But never try to shun the fray
And always seek the van of fight,
   And come the first, and "come to stay;"
      Needless a word in their behalf—
      We know the valor of the Staff!
In front of battle-lines they ride
To show the way—and, with a cheer,
The charging bayonets beside—
   Where glory is, the Staff is near!
      "Semper paratus" saith true sword:
      All honor to the golden cord!

Ah, comrades! relics of the war,—
   Baptized in blood and battle-stained;
The pride of every Army Corps
   Of record fame, what have you gained?—
      What your bounty, your reward?
      IN TIME OF PEACE AN UNTRIED SWORD!
This! for the Twelfth? Rest, gallant dead,
   So grandly sleeping, everywhere
That valor's richest blood was shed:
   Your glory HE shall never share!
      Only in peace, in foolish wrath,
      Silenus draws his sword of—lath!

NOTE.—"If this be treason, make the most of it."

JOHN THOMAS.

John Thomas was a roving blade
  Just sobered up from his last spree,
And, seeking for an easy trade,
  He chose the Fourth Artillery!
They dressed him up in Army blue,
  With pork and beans his belly filled;
The sergeant as all sergeants do,
  Had this recruit twice, daily, drilled.

John loved the Sutler's whisky, true—
  But found the "awkward squad" a bore;
Got sick of glory, through and through,
  And, hating peace, panted for war.
So, he decided to desert—
  Get drunk and have a lot of fun;
Sell out his "kit," to the last shirt,
  And make a raid on Washington.

He did; and took the "Avenue"
  With devious stride—so grapevine,
That all the brigadiers in blue,
  Whose single stars so brightly shine,
Abruptly scooped this soldier in;
  And put him in his little cell,
Until this vagrom man of sin
  His name and regiment could tell.

JOHN THOMAS.

When his first sober moment came
    They mustered him upon the slate,
And took him, weak, and sick, and tame,
    Before the Post Judge Advocate.
This Judge looked up the Rules of War—
    Prospected in that legal mine;
Then looked at John; and then he swore
    He'd broken all the "99!"

It took the Advocate one year
    To "specify" this soldier's crime;
He wrote, and wrote, and liv'd on beer—
    But smelled of whisky all this time!
'Twill take a Court one hundred more
    To try this complicated case;
To listen to the Judge's law
    And arguments, sure to take place—

To try John Thomas; and to find
    A proper punishment; for, he
Is a "dead-beat," the meanest kind;
    Recruit from the—Artillery!
"Go, soldier, to your honored rest!"
    But not to whence this "bummer" came,
If you seek glory, shun the nest
    That brought this loafer into fame.

Try the rough riders of the "horse,"
    They drink Artillerymen "Stone blind."
No half-foot-soldier can, of course,
    Drink square with heroes of their kind,—
Try the bold raiders of the Fifth—
    Who galloped after Sheridan!
Enlist with them; they have the "gift"
    For "laying out" Artillerymen.

Who ever drunk, a trooper saw—
    Who ever found his canteen full,
(Or his next neighbor's in the war,)
    If there was chance to "get a pull?"
John Thomas, join the mounted Corps,
    And ride, and drink in Phil's brigade;
They play the biggest game of draw
    The corks that ever mortals played!

Ad Valor—RUM.

The soldiers(?) who, with Wallace, bled
Our Uncle Samuel in war,
And fought with ink, the sword instead,
Now brag of fields they never saw.
Meanwhile the Nation, to this day,
Rewards them, for no daring done,
With old fogy and retired pay—
For never facing rebel gun.

No hero, daring death and wound,
Anticipated this sad hour,
When, marching from the battle-ground,
Quill-driving men should be in power.
Such, sympathy can never feel
For veterans of any grade,
Who with brave hearts and ready steel
Stood by their colors in brigade.

No tourist on the "Bloody James"
Shall find a record of them near.
No battle-field suggests the names
Of these bold heroes of the—Rear!
Yet, now, no dress-parade, review
But sees their martial forms divine,
Full of fuss, and feathers too,
Ferociously command the line.

The only "Johns" they ever met
    Are DEMI-johns of ancient rye;
The only "times" they care for yet,
    Are "good," and "old," and very "high."
Safe, in the rear, on soft detail,
    They vegetate in time of war,
But NOW the stoutest hearted quail
    When these fierce whisky lions roar.

Foolish the honors dearly bought,
    The glories of the great campaign;
The desp'rate battles bravely fought—
    This old "Home Guard" commands again!
Vain the laurel-wreathed crown,
    Won by the ever-ready sword—
In the great struggles for renown, .
    If peace but brings us THIS reward;—

Brings this disgrace to gallant men,
    Cruel is war, more cruel peace!
If swords are second to the pen,
    And eagles must be led by geese!
Many a loyal heart and brave
    Feels the truth in this sad story—
Better defeat, and nameless grave,
    Than this PEN—ultimate glory.

ASSES AND ASSES.

Balaam's rebuked his rider's sin;
   Sterne's unto him all good hearts drew:
Æsop's put on the lion's skin;
   Ohio's ass* a lion slew!
And that jealous state of Cass'
   (With no acre that is farmy)
Sent her pettifogging asses
   To "Militia" in the Army!.

Lord! let an angel again stand,
   As in the good old Balaam days,
Waiting two lawyers; in each hand
   Their briefless bags of old green baize.
So Michigan might have them back
   To their natural bent, good Lord;
Take soft "Dundreary" to old Zach,
   And Mizner with his jeweled sword!

O, Lord! the modern Philistine
   Laughs at these legal sprouts of war;
These Michiganders, assinine,
   Inherit not the Sampson jaw.
The ass that slew the lioness
   Died too young, but widely noted.
Mizner still lives, "pure cussedness,"
   To "boot-lick" and be promoted!

Lord, if the "Fool-killer" still kills,
    Take Craigie, ("Jenkins" of the mess!)
Purge the whole army of such ills;
    And so thy faithful soldiers bless.
Take all these men of small ideas,
    Give us again peace and accord;
Cast out this devil with long ears,
    From those who glorify the sword!

*At the Zoological garden, Cincinnati, Ohio, a donkey, upon being attacked by an escaped lioness, kicked her to death. Ohio, great in all her productions of men and other animals, gives this single example of a lion conquered by an ass qurdrupedal.

THE GREAT BATTLE OF THE WAR.
March 13th 1865.

You may talk of Look-out-Mountain,
And you may brag of Kenesaw,
Of the Wilderness and Gettysburg,
As "Most glorious" of the war.

You are very much mistaken
If you think the world forgets
The bloodiest battle of them all:—
That great struggle for brevets!

It was something providential,
For, when the recall was sounded,
And the mighty host was numbered,
Not an office-man was wounded!

Then boast of little Bunker's Hill,
And other victories, to me,
But the battle of the big brevets
Was the true Thermopylæ!

Then, to see the brave survivors
Riding home in sleeping-cars!
Their coats thrown carelessly about,—
To show NEW satelites of—Mars(?)

Hurrah, for the next war! hurrah!
May modest Bureau-crats contrive
To influence the big brevets,
As they all did in '65.

GEORGE(H)ICS,
The Drunken Man-at-Arms.

Hard drinking hath his face to scarlet turned;
  O, rum. too strong, O, water, never taken!
Whisky always this toper's vitals burned;
  And from its seat his reason ever shaken.
Brandy, rum, wine, "dutch courage" only give,
  Justice, truth, right, in temperance must live.

His record now—A SOLDIER OF THE PEN!
  Whose sword hath ever rusted in its sheath.
Never did he to battle lead his men;
  Having no heart to dare a soldier's death.
But though from "Active" to "Retired" he'll go,
  His pay is sure—ALL WON WITHOUT A BLOW.

And where he safely sits on office stool,
  He'll tell to clerks his awful deeds of might:
Brag of his own personal valor, cool
  In many a desperate, NAMELESS, fight.
Justice, how long shall this poor coward too
  Cumber the Army list; disgrace the blue?

MISCELLANEOUS PIECES.

MISCELLANEOUS PIECES.

SOME DAY.

Some day your soul will vainly pray
For the one, loyal love it knew,
But thinks so lightly of to-day—
The day repentance comes to you.
Some day—dishonor, and the shame
You glory in, will turn to lust;
And men will call you by a name
Bitter as death—bitter, but just.

Some day—the weak fool who now thinks
You altogether true, and his,
Will come to loathe you as he shrinks
From your false eyes and fatal kiss.
Some day will wake him from his dream—
To find you in another's arms;
And, to this other, you will seem
To bring unviolated charms.

Some day—the beauty of your face,
With all the loveliness of mien,
Will fade away, and that disgrace,
The "Scarlet letter," will be seen!
Some day—O, woman of deceit—
Falsehood in ev'ry wanton breath;
You shall come with reluctant feet,
Into a presence that is Death.

MISCELLANEOUS PIECES.

Some day—a day, alas, too late
To heal the broken hearts, and save
The life, you made so desolate,
From sorrow and a welcome grave—
Some day; when all seems to you lost,
With not one refuge you can see;
When you count up the fearful cost
Of all your sin; Remember me!

Some day—God will call you, too,
To His eternal judgment seat—
As Mary Magdalen, may you,
Through mercy, find a Savior's feet!
Some day? All days I humbly plead
That you may see the life you live;
That God may pardon you and lead
As I would lead you and forgive.

Some day, you will stand—all alone.
Beauty, youth, and health all wasted.
Of the forbidden fruits not one
But you have tasted and tasted
Some day—Fruits of your life's dead sea;
Bearing but ashes and decay—
Then, your unfaithfulness to me,
Will be your Nemesis—some day!

PERDIDA.

A girl—once sweet, and good, and fair—
Splendid and tender her gray eyes;
As stars in early morning skies—
Like Berenice's her brown hair.
She was beautiful—and sixteen.
My soul stirred at the lightest touch
Of her hands—for, I lov'd her much—
Truer loving never has been.

She was all tenderness, and sweet.
Only a school girl. With a grace
Of the Madonna, and her face—
But a nature full of deceit.
God made her fair, and sweet, and good;
But the world, and her evil ways,
Have soil'd her life—these many days;
And stain'd her soul and womanhood.

How the best feeling of my life
Went joyfully forth to meet her;
And my faith grew stronger, sweeter
For loving this maiden, and wife.
I wonder if she, sometimes, thinks
Of her truest of lovers yet;
And if, for this, she hides regret
For the past—in the cup she drinks—

Thinks of the patient heart, and brave,
Sorrowing at this ruin made;
Of loving hands so vainly laid
On her, in the attempt to save—
Too late to save from utter loss.
Yet, one escap'd God's death-shower:
One penitent, in the last hour,
Was pardon'd—even from the cross!

That one so beautiful—so young;—
A gracious life that might have been—
Should find all pleasures in a sin
That gives her shame to every tongue!
Now her old friends all pass her by—
None but the lost can see, can feel
The smile fade out, the look congeal,
The scorn in the averted eye.

She is outcast forevermore,
She is a false, and guilty thing.
For her no saving church bells ring,
No welcome at the chapel door,
No influence of home, of hearth,
Finds echo in her sordid heart—
From all of good she lives apart,
A Pariah by choice, and birth.

No mother's heart stirs within her
Whose life defiles the marriage vow;
No little children come, and bow
In prayer, unto this sinner.
Yet, she once was the pride, the boast
Of one whose soul knew her as queen—
Always, to him, she is sixteen!
To one she has betray'd the most.

Alas, the stealthy hand of time,
The changes wrought by gross excess,
Too surely mar all loveliness
That wakes in fear, and sleeps in crime!
Perdida—lost! O, God, how long
Shall run her terrible career?
This wreck of all the heart holds dear—
How long to suffer and be strong?

Note.—Perdida, signifies *lost*.

REST.

There is a consolation most profound,
  That seeks to dwell within my tortur'd breast;
I thought, sometime, my broken heart's rebound
  Had caught, at last, an interval of rest.
    But I could not enjoy the pain's surcease
    For thinking that her life had not found peace

For thinking that the idol I ador'd,
  To whom I gave a man's most sacred trust—
Had come to be, that wretched thing abhor'd,
  A desperate soul full of unbridl'd lust:
    Had brought dishonor on another's name
    By living out her heritage of shame.

Though my eyes may never look upon her,
  And never more her voice may reach my ear,
I know I held her in the greatest honor,
  As one most precious, beautiful, and dear.
    If God would turn her heart to what is best,
    And only good—then, I could be at rest.

Those are not the bitterest tears we shed
  Upon the marbles, and the grassy slope.
That mark the resting places of our dead;
  But where is buried all we had of hope.
    All our life-idols false lie broken here—
    Here vain grief must shed the bitterest tear.

Ah, if this woman's birthright had been chaste!
  What blessings to a hearthstone she might be:
And no man's life become a barren waste
  For loving, trusting her, so utterly.
    But hope is dead—my sun sinks in life's west:
    Alone I walk the path leading to rest.

NEMESIS.

Ever, the dread furies of Remorse
    Attend the evil way;
And time's swift revenges will enforce
    The forfeit sin must pay.

Some time, in supplication kneeling,
    You will be found at last,
In a vain agony appealing
    From your accusing Past.

Meanwhile, all the forbidden treasures,
    You eagerly pursue,
Will turn to bitter tasting pleasures—
    Forever cursing you.

Sinning, you can be gaining only
    The wages of your sin—
The mean death, and burial lonely,
    Of outcast gathered in.

Forward—hopeless desolation lies;
    Despairing days unblest.
Backward—the forsaken paradise
    Of honor and of Rest!

Bitter, the bondage of wilful shame—
    Ever the rod to kiss.
Always pursued by that sword of flame
    Nemesis—Nemesis!

TO-NIGHT.

O. my beloved! once again
   Tender arms with soft embraces
Have glorified my latest days;
   And blessed all my weary ways
With a splendor that effaces
   All my sufferings and my pain.

Never more can come to me
   Unhappiness; never more despair.
My soul is jubilant and strong;
   And the long silent, tender song
Of the olden time is there,
   The song I ever sang to thee.

Lovers may come to worship her,
   Many, may think her heart to win,
And lay their treasures at her feet.
   Never a one shall gain my sweet.
None but I can enter in
   And be her chosen minister.

I alone at the portal wait,
Like a priest at the temple door.
   With my faith in her heart of gold
Bringing a love that is new, and old.

A love that lives forevermore,
True and noble, just and great!

O, my beloved! you alone
  Hold in your gracious power
A life of earnest endeavor,
  The sweetness of time was forever
Born in that passionate hour,
  The last and the dearest—your own.

FAREWELL.

Farewell! and with your liberty
Take truest memories of me:
The long hours of my agony
Are not all past—though I am free.

My heart can never cease to beat
As fondly as it beat of yore;
My freedom can not be all sweet,
Since faith in you must live no more.

Should sorrow ever overtake,
And wound you, in your free career;
Think of the past— and, for my sake,
Live honestly; the life sincere!

Remember one whose heart alway
Was loyal, tenderest and true;
Who never wavered from that day
He gave himself to loving you.

No beauty can survive the years—
No loveliness, no outward grace.
When the sad heart holds hidden tears,
The signs will wear upon the face.

The brightest colors soonest fade,
And the most delicate perfume;
The sweetest flowers God has made
All early cease to bud and bloom.

So live, that when the Reaper's hand
Shall touch your life with fingers cold;
He will not find you shrinking stand—
Bound in your slavery of old!

Go! strive to be a woman pure—
Too proud to have a shame to tell.
I could forgive—were I but sure
Of your repentance true.   Farewell!

ONE WOMAN.

When one woman says she hates you,
Believe her not: look in her eyes!
And in her face of painted bloom,
And, when she swears she hates you,
Think of Saphira's righteous doom!
When this woman says she hates you
      She lies!

When one woman says she loves you,
Believe her not: look in her eyes!
And see the heartless treason there,
And, when she swears she loves you,
Think of slumbering Sampson's hair!
When this woman says she loves you
      She lies!

When one woman says she fears you,
Believe her not: look in her eyes!
They are not tender eyes, nor true,
And, when she swears she fears you,
Think of the life she must pursue!
When this woman says she fears you
      She lies!

When one woman says she trusts you,
Believe her not: look in her eyes!
And see the mocking devils shine.
And, when she swears she trusts you,
Think of your home deserted shrine!
When this woman says she trusts you
      She lies!

When one woman says she fools you,
Believe her, then! because, forsooth,
Of all the shameless front she wears.
And, when she swears she fools you
Think of her sad inheritance!
When swearing this, she truly swears
      The truth!

When one woman sees life ending,
And all her fascinating youth
Is wasted with excesses' fever:
She shall reap the harvest, bending
With the woes great sinnings leave her!—
For this woman lives offending
      All truth!

ONE LITTLE CORNER IN HER HEART.

To-morrow you will be nineteen.
  To-night, I hope that you will dream
Of one whose torment you have been.
  However little this may seem,
    It is a heavy cross—no less,
    To bear your want of tenderness.

I ask to have one little place—
  All mine—within your heart, in vain;
You promise "yes," then, turn your face
  And take the promise back again!
    Darling, was this fair, cheating so;
    To first, say yes, and last, say no?

You are a cruel tyrant, sweet,
  Wounding a tender heart and true—
The lover lying at your feet
  Deserves a better fate from you:
    A fairer recompense than this—
    A gracious yes, at least—a kiss!

Good night, my darling and my queen;
  Good night, sweetheart and love, good night.
To-morrow—you will be nineteen.
  God grant you many birthdays bright;
    And keep, for me alone—apart,
    One little corner in your heart!

WITH ROSES.

Sweet, with every bud, I send
    A wish for all of human bliss
To be with you unto the end:
    With ev'ry leaf I send—a kiss.

I saw my roses on your breast,
    And envied their sweet lot, to-night;
And wished the giver were as blest—
    So near the paradise in sight!

Were I the roses, I would kiss
    The dimple in that charming chin;
The darling mouth I would not miss,
    But kiss ten thousand kisses in.

Mistakes will happen in the hours
    When all is blended, in the shade;
Your fragrant lips seemed my flowers—
    And mine for tasting sweets were **made!**

"To err is human"—I confess;
    But the temptation was divine!
I ask no greater happiness
    Than to repeat this sin of mine.

A saint elect would not repent
    This larceny of sweets sublime.
Therefore am I impenitent:
    Asking no mercy for this crime!

THE TRUE WIFE.

God knows my lonely life is sad—
  Knows the sore pain and bitter cost
Of all the fleeting pleasures had,
  Since the true hearted one was lost.
Though she is gone from mortal eye
  She is not ever dead to me,
Always I feel her mercies nigh;
  Always one loving face I see.

God has this bounty to us shown;
  When dire affliction falls on men,
Some tender, truest life-love known
  Comes to console and comfort then.
So comes to me, faithful and true,
  My truest friend—the loyal wife!
Her loving office to renew,
  And teach me of the better life.

Ah! if we knew the pain in store
  That sorrows bring us, day by day;
We could not struggle for that shore
  That ever fades, and fades away.
Thank God! beyond there ever stands
  One watcher, always waiting me,
With loyal heart, and faithful hands
  To bear me on life's stormy sea.

PARTING.

Hold out thy gracious hands and bless me,
  O, my beloved! take me to your heart;
I fain would linger to caress thee—
  To tell thee all my loving ere we part.
Let me, sitting at your feet, forgetting sadness,
Speak of our future meetings and tender gladness.

For time will soothe your mournful feeling,
  And surely bring the returning hour near,—
What treasures Time is always stealing
  When you are absent, and I, lonely here.
What dreary days of waiting, and what cruel pain,
Will be my torture to the hour we meet again.

Think of me waiting for you, lonely—
  Not one thy loving kindness to replace;
Think that I sigh for, love you, only,
  And cannot look upon my dear one's face.
My darling, think of me when evening stars appear,
Steadfast as worlds, beloved, I am waiting here.

My loving soul, these arms outreaching,
  Will hold thee ever tenderly and true;
All hours without thee will be teaching
  Some gentle souvenir of you.
God bless you, my beloved! partings there must be,
But in your joyous, happiest hours, think of me.

Cling round my neck detaining fingers;
   Eyes see in eyes positive conviction.
I am as one that goes, yet lingers
   For one more kiss, one last benediction.
As one whose cruel chain and captive fate deny
The fruit so near his hungry soul and thirsty eye.

Delay me still, hide my emotion
   In the brown splendor of thy tangled hair;
I bring thee that supreme devotion
   No time, no distance can impair.
Release me from these binding tresses—set me free;
When other voices praise their glory, think of me.

ASK NOT THIS HEART.

Ask not this loyal heart
To tell of all its trust and hope in thee:
To speak the useless words, to tear apart
And break the voiceless spell—Fidelity.
Seek for these deathless truths within my eyes—
Seek there replies.

Count the bright sands and stars, so numberless,
That belt the seas and stud the shining blue:
All these reach not the sum of tenderness
And trust it feels for you.
Sooner than love, the restless waves will tire—
These worlds on fire.

Ask not if I forget.
The silent stars will move on—forever;
The sands will ever be by oceans wet:
And I change not. Unto me can never
Come a new love, and martyrdom of pain—
Never again.

Impatience for the lingering morrow
Will soothe no anguish of the long to-day;
Think of my weary solitude and sorrow;
Pitying me, alway.
Ask not this heart if faith in you is fled—
I am not dead.

DEAD.
Under Two Flags.

Gather the dead from battle fields
And bear them to the chosen ground;
Gather the broken swords and shields,
And pile them on the battle mound.
>Dead, for the banner set with stars:
>Our birthright glory crown'd with years:
>Dead, for the ephemeral "bars,"
>Heavy with blood and woman's tears.

O, still and grand the legions keep
Their steadfast ranks the breastwork nigh:
The North and South together sleep;
Teaching the world how heroes die.
>Die, for one banner bright with stars;
>A nation's emblem all these years:
>Die, for the other crossed with bars,
>Torn and bloody, lost in tears.

Under this green and grassy mound,
Camping with death, in equal graves,
Men of the South and North are found,
Above them all one splendor waves!
>Waves, in beauty, the stripes and stars:
>Waves, the glorious gift of years:
>Over the dead, from lofty spars,
>Waving for all, one flag appears.

Gather the dead and valient sons
Our country gave to glory there;
The mighty voice of minute guns
Shall tell their number to the air.
 Tell, their number under the stars;
 Under the stripes splendid of yore:
 Splendid with freedom's battle-scars—
 Under the flag WASHINGTON bore.

Sadly, from separate regions,
AMERICA gathers them here:
Gathers the dead of her legions—
From encampments of glory near.
 Sadly, her standard is throwing
 A shadow of pride on their bed:
 And the bugles of sorrow are blowing
 A mournful tattoo, for her dead.

MISCELLANEOUS PIECES.

ONLY THEE.

Only thee—pure angel of the Lord—
To smile the sorrow of this world away;
With gentle, pleading ways and words, to say—
"Live but for me—put away the sword!"
Only thee—to worship and adore;
To look upon as wholly, truly mine;
To have no thought, no wish, no life not thine,
No lost hope your love may not restore.

Only thee— teaching a faith sublime;
While the swift years, with busy fingers, trace
A life's stern record on my fading face—
All youth's history and manhood's prime;
Teaching me to look above and see
The promise of a purer, better land;
Leading me by the heart—and, hand in hand
Walking the thorny ways,—only thee!

Only thee— patient of soul and heart;
Sweet in the innocence of girlish faith;
Whose life, unto me eloquently saith,
"Here is the right way—the better part."
Whose constant prayer is but a plea
That some beneficence shall daily fall
Upon me. Who loveth and forgiveth all;
Forgiving and loving—even me!

Only thee—joy for all life's sorrow,
And tender refuge from all earthly grief,
The great foundation rock of my belief,
That death to-day, is life to-morrow.
That the old, decaying, blasted tree—
Death in its sapless branches, trunk and roots,
Like Aaron's rod will blossom, and bear fruits,
In Lands you promise me—only thee.

Only thee—on your suppliant knees;
Pleading for me at the gates of glory—
Telling to the Savior all my story.
Yes, "His Kingdom is of such as these!"
And, when the great voices, calling me,
Shall bid me come and walk with death,
Be near me then; receive my parting breath;
Show me that fruitful land—only thee.

IN CHURCH.

Farewell, dear maiden, with the tender eyes,
 God bless that bright sunshine hair and face,
You made my station here a paradise,
 And gave my heart a happy resting place.
God bless you now, and farewell, my dear;
 You that made blessed every moment here.

THE LAST.

To one last haven doth the pilot steer,
   To anchor in some quiet bay.—
The soldier turns from one last glory dear
   And casts his broken sword away.

One seeks the ever peaceful shore, secure
   From ocean's stormy winds and wave:
No more the bugle's battle calls allure
   The other to a nameless grave.

What is the influence that surely draws
   The sailor to the smiling land—
The eager soldier from a nation's wars?
   Only a loving woman's hand.

To one last tenderness I give my heart,
   To one last hope my all of life.
I must be wreck'd if this last anchor part
   And drift me from my "darling wife."

TO ——

Oh! if my weary head might rest
    Upon such heavenly delight—
Pillowed on that distracting breast
    And dream in paradise to-night!
My soul deliciously would lie
    Enchanted by my darling's charms,
Content to live, even to die—
    First in her heart; last in her arms.

In life or death God knoweth well
    The tenderest of love I feel;
No anchorite in holy cell
    With truer faith can ever kneel—
Yes, if I die with all this bliss
    Slow fading from my closing eyes,
My hope shall be to meet, to kiss
    Her as an angel in the skies.

Surely the souls united here
    Shall meet above in love again,
I wish no resurrection, dear,
    If such a gentle hope is vain.
Better the dark and hopeless creed
    Resolving all unto the earth—
Even the plants have winged seed,
    To bear them to a higher birth.

No mortal happiness and griefs
  But carry memories beyond
The border lines of such beliefs—
  And lovers true never despond,
But serve, and trust, and hope, and wait.
  Knowing that at the end of time
Ever stands the immortal's gate
  Opening to the life sublime.

IN CHURCH.

How this dull parson's drowsy monotones
  Seem but to justify the deacon's snore.
My blood is stagnant, and my very bones
  And martyred flesh are suffering sore.
If 'twere not for your tenderest look
  And the fondness of your sympathizing face:
I would let drop my misty seeming book,
  And, with the deacon, fall away from grace.

Christ's Church—Elmira, N. Y.

Farewell, Elmira, lovely town, adieu!
  Good-bye to all sweethearts in this church.
May those who follow us and rent this pew,
  Pay up as prompt and leave no one in lurch.
Ah! darlings, if we could only stay—
  But soldiers love, and love, and march away.

www.ingramcontent.com/pod-product-compliance
Lightning Source LLC
Chambersburg PA
CBHW020145170426
43199CB00010B/890